ATTRACT FAMILIES

TO YOUR CHURCH

AND KEEP THEM COMING BACK

Praise for *Attract Families to Your Church
and Keep Them Coming Back*

"Families today look much different than twenty years ago. What Linda has put together provides a road map for the church not only to minister to today's families but also to meet their needs and be relevant in their lives. Drawing from a unique understanding of the social and psychological challenges facing families, this book is a must read for anyone seeking to attract families as a means of serving their local community."

—**Michael Chanley**, Executive Director of the International Network of Children's Ministry (INCM), Founder of CMConnect

"The gospel is relevant for every generation, every culture, and every family. But if we—the church—can't connect to today's family, we can't share the gospel with them. *Attract Families* will open your eyes and your heart and equip your church to engage people where they live."

—**Ron L. Deal**, author of *The Smart Stepfamily*; RonDeal.org

"Linda Jacobs writes from a wealth of experience, offering keen insight along the way, as she is motivated from a heart of compassion. Every pastor and church leader who is serious about reaching their community for Jesus should prayerfully read this book."

—**Tom Ravan**, Pastor, First Baptist Church of Bessemer City, North Carolina

"How does a church stay relevant and influential in a fast changing society? With decades of experience, Linda Jacobs gives us new, innovative and practical ideas any church can implement right away!"

—**Eric & Jennifer Garcia**, Cofounders, Association of Marriage and Family Ministries

"Linda Ranson Jacobs has her hand on the pulse of the church. Pastor and church leaders who want to make sure their churches stay healthy need to read this book. She brilliantly defines the problem and solutions for the church as they maximize their ministry to the challenges of today's families."

—**Scott Turansky**, Cofounder, National Center for Biblical Parenting

ATTRACT FAMILIES

TO YOUR CHURCH

AND KEEP THEM COMING BACK

LINDA RANSON JACOBS

 Abingdon Press™

Nashville

ATTRACT FAMILIES TO YOUR CHURCH AND KEEP THEM COMING BACK

This book is printed on acid-free paper.

Library of Congress Cataloging-in-Publication Data

Jacobs, Linda Ranson.
  Attract families to your church and keep them coming back / Linda Ranson Jacobs.
    pages cm
  Includes bibliographical references.
    ISBN 978-1-4267-7430-0 (pbk. : alk. paper) 1. Church work with families. 2. Evangelistic work. I. Title
  BV4438.J33 2014
  259'.1—dc23

                                                                    2013036765

14 15 16 17 18 19 20 21 22 23—10 9 8 7 6 5 4 3 2 1
MANUFACTURED IN THE UNITED STATES OF AMERICA

Contents

Acknowledgments

I wish to acknowledge the hundreds of people who have impacted my ministry and my life down through the years. Your faces and your stories are ever before me. The single moms and dads, the struggling blended-family parents, the boomerang parents, the grandparents parenting another generation, and, of course, the children and teens have all contributed to the development of this book.

Chapter 1

The Church That Might Have Been

The LORD will guide you always;
he will satisfy your needs in a sun-scorched land
and will strengthen your frame.
You will be like a well-watered garden,
like a spring whose waters will never fail.

—Isaiah 58:11

There she was, a large church in a metropolitan city right in the middle of the Bible Belt. The steps, cascading from her front door down to the sidewalk and the manicured grounds, were magnificent. This church was a beautiful building with ornate designs on the outside. The sanctuary was elegant and had a huge pipe organ, upholstered pews, a large pulpit and choir loft, and beautiful wooden beams overhead. There were also several large parking lots attached to the property of this church.

The playground was well furnished. As a matter of fact, there were several playgrounds. There was a nice well-equipped gym for the children, with basketball goals and other equipment that teens and adults could use. There was also a well-furnished, up-to-date commercial kitchen.

Every day during the week, the church was filled with more than one hundred children. Laughter filled the rooms. Joyful sounds, music, and excitement could be felt around the church building. Infants, toddlers, and preschoolers lived in these rooms Monday through Friday in the church-sponsored preschool program.

Parents came in and out of this church building from early Monday morning until 6:00 p.m. on Friday evening. When one adds in all the staff it takes to care for over a hundred children, you can imagine all of the people who had access to this beautiful church building every week.

On Sunday when the childcare was closed and church services were held, this church had a grand total of twelve members. Twelve people! Even though the church building met all the state codes, including the fire code and health code, and met city building standards, there really was no church—only an almost-empty building every Sunday.

What Happened to This Church?

Down through the years the church members had moved to outlying communities and suburbs and changed their membership to churches in these new areas. Or the children had grown up and moved away, while the older generation gradually died off. The only way the church could survive was to lease its building to a childcare and preschool program. The saddest part of this story was that there was already an entire church within this building and the membership of the church didn't recognize it. The building was filled to the brim five days a week with a lot of nontraditional families and even some traditional two-parent families, but most of the two-parent families were lower income and not what the church was used to having (or wanting) as its membership.

While the church's members might have moved, left town, or died, there was a newer generation of

- single parents,
- children living with grandparents,

- stepfamilies and blended families, and
- lower-income two-parent families.

And all of these families were using the church building five days a week. However, none of the church members saw the potential of reaching out and re-creating the church's emphasis. Perhaps it was stubbornness. Or maybe the elderly members couldn't bring themselves to accept these different kinds of families worshiping in their church on Sunday.

Whatever the reason, the members of this church missed an opportunity to create a new kind of worship experience and an opportunity to explode the kingdom of God with new converts. This sad commentary is all too common in other churches as well.

We see and hear about many churches in similar situations, while many ministers and congregations are searching for new converts and members. Many simply don't know how to go about making the changes needed to update or re-create their church. I'm not saying that doctrine needs to be changed or theology needs to be compromised or negotiated. But what is evident, though, is that in order for churches in our country to survive they need to change and shift their emphasis to new kinds of ministry if they want to attract families and keep them coming back.

If you are part of a church that is seeking to attract church members and grow, perhaps you might want to take a look at the community where your church is located. Are you like the "Church That Might Have Been"? Do you want to grow by adding new families? Has your community changed over the years? Do you need to refocus your attention on different types of families? Or perhaps you need to look out the windows of your church to see the various cultures and ethnic groups that have moved into your community.

If we want to build our church membership today, and if we want to preserve the church of the future, we need to look at where our communities are and what kinds of families are in our communities. It is not about programs or gimmicks. It is about families. It is about relationships. It is about reaching out and sharing the love of Christ to a new and different generation in a culturally diverse and ever-changing world.

David T. Olson, the author of *The American Church in Crisis*, says,

> The ongoing downturn in church attendance this millennium is partially related to external cultural changes. Many of the people in the emerging culture do not share the philosophical assumptions of 50-year-old churches or even of churches that are just 20 year old. Largely unaware of these changes, many churches continue to operate in modes and mentalities that no long resonate with our culture.[1]

Think about some of the various types of churches, programs, and cycles we've experienced over the last couple of generations:

- Bus ministries. While not as large as they were during the 1980s, some churches still have successful bus ministries.
- TV and Internet churches
- House churches
- Store-front, small start-up churches that expect to grow into megachurches. Some have been successful at this.
- Megachurches like Willow Creek Community Church in South Barrington, Illinois; Saddleback Community Church in Lake Forest, California; The Potter's House in Dallas, Texas; Lakewood Church in Houston, Texas; and Life Church in Oklahoma City, Oklahoma
- Small-group Bible studies

All of these are valuable and good for the population they are meant for, but not every person wants to

- belong to a large megachurch;
- be in a small, intimate, group Bible study;
- attend a video service in a location away from the main speaker every week;
- be in or feel comfortable in a small or midsize church; or
- put their child on a bus to go to a church several miles away.

A church that wants to enlarge their membership is going to have to figure out how to connect with the people in their community. That means researching and finding out exactly who is in your community:

1. If you want to know about your community, talk to the public schools. They will have a good handle on what kinds of families are in your community.

2. Go to the service agencies. Who do they serve or reach out to? Is it low income, military, foster care families, single parents?

3. Check with the local Chamber of Commerce to see how it expects your community to grow in the next few years. Does it know of a particular kind of business or a special group of people it will be trying to attract in the future?

4. Check with your own denomination's head office or research team. Many denominations have predictions you can glean information from to take back to your elders, deacons, or focus groups.

For years when people who did not attend church on a regular basis experienced a crisis or had a problem, they would search out a minister or a local church. Church used to be the mainstay in communities. That is no longer true. We have brought up an entire generation that was not raised in church. They no longer think of church as the first place to go to for help. They go to a secular psychologist or therapist. They might even indulge in a new religion, one that doesn't believe in Jesus Christ. They turn to the Internet, TV, and social media.

All of us are seriously going to have to find ways to bring the lost into the local church. Many of us are going to have to venture outside our comfort zones in order to reach the generation that doesn't consider church to be a valuable option for life problems. Let's go back to the "Church That Might Have Been" and see what they could have done.

Some Suggested Solutions

What if this church had held a VBS in the evenings and held sessions for the parents also? It could have been a stepping-stone to bring some of these families into the church family.

What if this church had started a Sunday morning "family" class where nontraditional and traditional families were allowed to worship together or at least all read the same scripture each week? Family discussion questions could be e-mailed each week to discuss what each family member had learned about that week's lesson.

What if there were a single-dad support group where dads who had full custody, part-time custody, or only had their children for visitation a couple of times a month could learn how to parent alone and come together for support, for fellowship, and to encourage one another?

What if this church had invested in some single-parenting seminars to help single moms with parenting skills?

What if they held some classes on how to successfully create a stepfamily? Single parents wanting to marry could then receive training in how to blend their new family.

Or newly blended families could come together and be taught how to strengthen their marriage and parent the children together.

Could some two-parent families use some sessions on strengthening their marriage and maybe even some parenting workshops? Perhaps the church could bring in special speakers to help in this area.

What if the church developed a car-care ministry, food pantry, or a clothes closet for the single moms? And what if the single moms volunteered in exchange for the services?

What if some financial classes were held and traditional two-parent families, blended families, and single parents were taught wise money management?

What if this church hosted small-group classes or special support programs? Some examples are

- GriefShare (www.griefshare.org),
- DivorceCare (www.divorcecare.org),

- DivorceCare for Kids, (www.dc4k.org),
- Celebrate Recovery Support groups (www.celebraterecovery
  .com/), and
- Single & Parenting (www.singleandparenting.org).

What about the grandparents who are parenting the second and even third generations? Don't they deserve some support, encouragement, and even some help for their tired bodies?

Let's not forget the "sandwich generation." These are the people caught in between or sandwiched between raising their children and caring for elderly parents or grandparents. These people are exhausted. They are barely able to attend a traditional Sunday service, and if the truth were known, many probably doze through the service. However, they want to be fed. They need to connect with God and they need encouragement from their church family, even if it is only on Sunday mornings.

Another currently growing segment of our population is the boomerang generation. These are the single adults who have graduated from college or tech school who have come back home to roost until they can find a job and get on their feet. Some are also divorced adults trying to get back on their feet. Many don't attend church, and yet they, too, deserve the church's attention.

These are only a few of the different types of families and people that a church can reach out to in our world. Church attendance should matter to us as Christians today. There are plenty of people in our communities but church attendance is declining.

From *The American Church in Crisis* by David T. Olson, we read, "When church attendance declines, fewer people hear the gospel for the first time, take the sacraments, or hear of God's love for them. Fewer marriages are restored. Fewer teenagers find a listening ear. The question of 'How many people attend church?' matters deeply because people matter."[2]

What if this church of just twelve people had prayed and earnestly sought the Lord's design for a different kind of vibrant church in that metropolitan area? Maybe, just maybe, more souls could have been brought into the Kingdom. More hurting people could have found peace and contentment in the Word. Perhaps some would have latched onto a joy-filled church family to replace the family they lost along the way.

Church Is Important in Our World

I firmly believe in church. I love going to church. I find contentment and joy being in church and worshiping with church family. Many times I have found myself bowing my head in the sanctuary of a church and just being in fellowship with the Father. Other people and sounds become oblivious to me when I'm with the Father. To me the church is God's dwelling place. It is God's home and his temple in my world today.

Over the years I have done a lot of different things and had a lot of different roles in churches. I've had an unusual vantage point to observe the inner workings of a church. For almost fifty years I have been a church pianist, organist, keyboardist, and accompanist in churches across the United States. I have served in all sizes of churches, including large churches, midsize churches, and small rural churches. I've served in churches in large metropolitan areas such as San Diego, California, and in small rural areas such as Youngsville, North Carolina.

Because ministers and I spend a lot of time together in the sanctuary getting ready for services, I usually develop a good relationship with the church staff. Because many times I am visible in front of the congregation, I develop a solid relationship with many members of the church. When I remember someone's favorite hymn or praise and worship song, or his or her loved one's favorite songs, those casual relationships grow deeper. And because I've played for hundreds of funerals and weddings, I have developed an intimate relationship with many congregants. After developing a ministry to the hurting and to single parents, I've been invited to speak all over the United States and Canada in various denominations. Almost weekly I hear from church leaders in other countries as well. With the popularity of social media, connecting with others in ministry in other parts of the world has become easier.

Over the years I've learned what attracts different people to church. I've also learned what sends some of them screaming away from a church family. I've heard stories that would curl your hair. I've prayed for congregations and prayed with ministers and individual servants that they would find their calling. I've laughed, cried, and shared many moments of joy.

The Lord has seen fit to allow me to pull strength from trials and tribulations in my own life. The Lord has been good to me in keeping my desire to be with him alive and strong. I grew up in church and I hope to die going to church. I believe church is only a prelude to how wonderful sitting at the feet of Jesus is going to be. Do you get the picture that I love church?

I've also started a church preschool and later worked as a children's ministry director in a church in Oklahoma. I have gotten close to the families through the children. I currently serve as coordinator of Adult Care Ministries at a church in Florida.

Like I said, I have had a very unusual position to observe the church for many years. Throughout this book I will share true scenarios and give you the benefit of a wealth of experience and success for growing churches.

You Don't Know What You Don't Know

Our world is changing rapidly. With the advent of many new technologies, connecting with the people in our communities should be easier. Older people are living longer and babies continue to be born daily. With better health care and new advances in medicine, children who would have died years ago are surviving. In the United States, immigrants are arriving at staggering rates. And yet our overall church attendance in America is declining.

Thom Shultz in the Holy Soup blog entitled "5 Ways the Church Will Change" presents the question, "Is the American church fading away? Will the losses in membership and attendance lead to a marginalized church presence such as that in the present-day Europe?"[3]

There is much all of us can do to prevent the American church from fading into oblivion:

- It may mean we change the way we think.

  1. We have been in a new millennium for several years now with new electronic devices and new ways of communicating and new ways to reach out, but many churches still operate as though they were back in the early nineties with phone calls and unannounced visits to prospective members.

  2. Society and even laws have changed.

  3. Do you know what is happening in the state, city, and community surrounding your church building?

- It may mean we have to study and keep up-to-date on research on the lifestyles that have evolved over the past generation.

  1. Are you aware of the number of people parenting alone in your community?

  2. Do you realize many more children are being parented by grandparents?

  3. Are you aware that many of the grandparents parenting the second generation are divorced or in a blended family? This means they may be older, exhausted, and less patient while they parent alone. If it is a blended family, it means one of the grandparents is not related to these children by blood. It is difficult to form a relationship and discipline a child you don't know. Many grandparents tell me they worked hard to raise their own children to be successful young adults, and now they are "stuck" with parenting young children whose parents are not capable of parenting. Others tell me they resent having to raise someone else's grandkids when it interferes with spending time with their own grandchildren.

4. What about cohabitating couples? Will your church be prepared to minister and speak biblical truths to them in love?

- It might mean we have to rethink what church looks like to the younger generation.

    1. The younger generations are screen junkies. Most are attached to their mobile devices and this may mean we do children's ministries differently by using some of the new technologies. It may mean using games and stories using screens and mobile devices.

    2. Will your congregation be able to accept the fact that young people might be reading the scriptures on their mobile device instead of a printed Bible held in their hands or taken from the pew rack in front of them? Or they might take notes on their mobile device. Perhaps they are checking on the accuracy or the pastor's facts and resources.

    3. Young people need relationships and deep connections with others. Younger men who were raised in a single-mom home need older male mentors to help them learn how to parent from a father's perspective.

- It may mean you look out the front doors of your church to see the various ethnic groups that have moved into your community.

    1. Ethnic diversity is everywhere. Gone are the days when ethnic groups met only with people of their group and away from other groups. Cultural and ethnic groups are merging in churches across America.

    2. Some churches hold English-as-a-second-language classes and encourage people of various nationalities to join in worship.

3. Other churches embrace cultural diversity by expanding their emphasis on missions within their own community.

I now attend a church in northwest Florida. We have a high military concentration and consequently our church is full of people from many different cultures. Many have moved to the United States with a military spouse. I love attending church with so many people groups. I enjoy sitting behind the Portuguese women when they sing and sway to the praise music. I enjoy watching the older African American women come into our church all decked out with their hats and scarves. And when the British people speak, I relish in their accent. I have two Filipino friends and I like to listen to them as they talk about the Philippines and how they found Jesus Christ in America. All of these people blend into our worship. What a joy to experience a loving God together in his house.

Perhaps your community doesn't have as many different nationalities as we are privileged to have in our community, but I imagine there is at least one other culture that you are not aware is living in your community. Do some research to find out what groups of people are living near your church. You might find an entire community just waiting to be invited to join your church family.

- It could mean that you ask someone else to head up a ministry to those in life crisis if you haven't personally experienced something similar.

  1. Addictive behaviors are becoming the norm in our society. Are you aware of the people in your congregation who have overcome a particular addiction (pornography, gambling, alcohol, drugs, and so on) and can help others?

  2. In a *Christianity Today* article we learn that many young adults struggle with addictions to a substance: "It appears that half of twenty-somethings today may battle some form of addiction. The church can't

be caught flat-footed if we want to see a generation redeemed."[4]

3. Depression because of job loss and other losses needs to be addressed in practical terms.

4. Divorcing adults need support recovery groups.

5. People who have lost a loved one because of terminal illness, suicide, or an accident all need support and recovery help.

Realize and admit that you don't know what you don't know. What do I mean by that? A life crisis such as divorce is a good example regarding this statement. I have ministers tell me all the time, "I don't need to have been divorced to understand divorce." Do you have any idea of the number of divorced people who leave the church? I do, because I minister to them. Many want to stay involved in church. They yearn to belong to a church family, but countless divorced people have told me, "I feel like I have *divorced* written across my forehead." On the topic of divorce you kind of do need to have been divorced, been reared in a divorced home, or have some personal experience with divorce to truly understand it and be able to empathize with people dealing with it.

Death of a mate is another crisis that one has to experience to truly understand it. I'm not saying you can't preach or teach on these subjects, but to truly understand what the person left behind is feeling and experiencing, you have to have experienced it in some way. Or others in the church family need to have a personal experience with it in order to be able to connect to the hurting in your congregation.

When my father passed away I felt sorry for my mother. I thought I really knew what she experienced in her grief, in her loneliness, and even in her anger. But it wasn't until my own husband died of cancer that I truly knew what she went through. My older sister and her husband divorced, and, again, I felt for her. I sympathized with her. I prayed for her; but until my husband left and divorced me, I didn't really understand all of the nuances involved in healing from that crisis. I didn't know what I didn't know.

It was after I experienced a divorce that this scripture caught my attention and helped me understand why I needed to be empathetic to people in crisis: "Praise be to the God and Father of our Lord Jesus Christ, the Father of compassion and the God of all comfort, who comforts us in all our troubles, so that we can comfort those in any trouble with the comfort we ourselves receive from God. For just as we share abundantly in the sufferings of Christ, so also our comfort abounds through Christ" (2 Corinthians 1:3-5).

People who have experienced a crisis can minister to others going through the same thing often better than the pastor can, simply because they have experienced it. I have been comforted by Christ and by these Christian friends. They knew which scripture I needed on which day. They knew what to say in particular situations. They helped me heal in places I didn't even know I was injured. They have walked in my shoes.

One of the pastors I've worked with has studied divorce. He sympathizes with the divorced person and his or her children. He prays for them and he loves them. He is a wonderful minister with a huge heart for the hurting, but he doesn't truly get all that is involved in being divorced. For many pastors, divorce is messy, and they get frustrated by the continual crying, arguing, and moaning that can accompany the beginnings of divorce recovery.

Divorce recovery is a new ministry for this church. We are just completing our first year and our third thirteen-week support group this year. My minister and others in the church are beginning to see how the hurting are being helped. They are rejoicing in seeing changed lives in the Lord. The people outside our church who have started attending because of our divorce recovery program have also surprised our congregation. Our divorce group is beginning to attend church worship services. They are connecting with others in the church, and some are venturing into serving in other ministries.

Now other members in our church are beginning to think outside the box. They are beginning to research other ways to reach out to the people in our community. All of this is because the head minister, other ministers, and church leaders were wise enough and willing to allow someone who had been comforted by the Father of compassion and the God of all comfort, who comforts us in all our troubles, to comfort those in any trouble in our community.

Look outside your church and start asking the hard questions about the people in your community. In the book *Transformational Church*, Ed Stetzer and Thom S. Rainer say we need to ask the following questions:

- Who lives here?
- What are their hurts?
- What are their dreams?
- Where do they spend their time?
- How do they relate to one another?[5]

I would like to add one more question to the list:

- What are their stories?

Everyone has a story. Find out what people's stories are and explore to see if you can become part of their story.

The Decline of Churches

The decline of churches is receiving a lot of attention from the research field. Denominations are worried. Ministers are concerned. Even policy makers and politicians are concerned about the weakening role churches play in our country. Many have concluded that there is a correlation between churches' disappearing role in the community and the vanishing of traditional families.

In 1969 I moved to California to join my navy husband. I had just graduated from college and was full of ideas, hopes, and dreams. Growing up in middle America, I had not been exposed to divorce. Divorce only happened to the movie stars in Hollywood. Shortly after I arrived in California, Governor Ronald Reagan signed the no-fault divorce law. Divorce seemed to take off like a speeding bullet, and it was aimed at the families of America.

Divorce became rampant in the 1970s, and it began to affect every area of community life:

- Schools began to see out-of-control and stressed children.
- Childcare began to experience challenging behavior in their infant, toddler, and preschool rooms.
- Churches began to see the divorced quietly walk out the back door of the church.
- Unaccompanied teens started searching out others who were left alone and unsupervised and they began to form gangs.
- Teenage pregnancy rates increased.
- Teenage suicides were on the rise.
- Dropout rates from high schools increased.
- Younger and younger children began to drink and use drugs.[6]

We now have two generations that experienced the divorce of their parents. Many of these adult children of divorce no longer attend church. The reason? Many single divorcing parents left the church because they no longer felt worthy of attending church; they felt guilty, they felt judged, or they may have been simply too tired.

Divorce not only changed the landscape of families in America, but it changed the landscape of churches also. Now society and our churches are facing the downturn and loss of the traditional families and family values in our country.

What Do We Do Now?

- Churches can be resilient if reliance on the Lord is maintained.
- Churches can survive when they bow the knee in prayer.
- Churches can and will move forward in the future when they evaluate trends and develop solution strategies.

In November of 2012, Group Publishing hosted "The Future of the Church Summit."[7] They brought together church leaders, denominational executives, and religion researchers to discuss and come up with some strategies and suggestions. They evaluated current trends and came up with some predictions about the church of the future.

I've heard other people discuss many of these trends, and I had already come to many of the same conclusions myself long ago. For instance, many of these experts talked about the rise of using volunteers more and paid ministers less. This makes sense since churches are struggling with our reduced economy. Many churches have seen reduced giving with congregants out of work or just struggling to survive themselves. Churches that are not hiring new staff will have to rely on unpaid ministry workers if they want to reach the hurting in their communities.

Another concept that is becoming more and more popular, and one the summit concluded to be important, is "relationship building." In the past, attending church merely meant being a spectator. The person came on Sunday morning, sang a few songs from the hymnbook, filled out a visitor's slip, listened to the preacher, shook a few hands, and walked out the door.

People want relationships. Relationships matter. People want to connect and they want to matter. If you are not a Christian or a regular church attendee and you walk into a church, it can be a frightening experience. You don't really know how to act or what is expected of you. If there is someone there you can connect with immediately, you are more likely to come back. When someone takes the time to find out about you and hear a little of your story, you connect with that person.

Other conclusions and predictions the summit members published are:

- Return to Jesus. The current church is preoccupied with the "ABCs"—attendance, buildings, and cash. The coming church will highly focus its mission, goals, measurements, and message on Jesus.

- Community focus. The church of tomorrow will be much more engaged in addressing the needs of the community. The church will be known more for its members' relational acts of compassion outside of the church walls, taking ministry out rather than waiting for outsiders to come in and sit.

I have one more idea:

- Churches will need to bind together in a local community effort. Instead of competing, church ministries may need to come together in support of one another and for the blending of resources.

For several years I was the national trainer for DivorceCare for Kids (DC4K) with Church Initiative. When our organization would go into an area to do training for DivorceCare, DC4K, and Grief-Share, several churches would come together to support the training event. Denominational walls came down. Camaraderie, laughter, and sharing became the highlights of the day. The event was always held in a local church and other churches would be invited to bring their volunteers for training.

In our training events we saw strong support develop between those people who attended together. It didn't matter what the name of their church was or what denomination they belonged to when these volunteers came together to support one another, to train together, to share their stories, and to pray for one another and the hurting in their community. Some areas created a local network fellowship group where the support continued year-round. One could call any church in that area and it would have a schedule of what day other churches were meeting. The call to minister to the hurting knows no competition or boundaries in those communities. Hurting people benefit, and the kingdom of God increases.

Churches are going to have to embrace societal change. Many churches are trapped in the last century and in particular the 1970s, 1980s, and 1990s. Their congregations are still arguing about singing hymns with a choir and organ or rejoicing with praise songs, a key-board, and a praise team. We have moved beyond that argument.

In the book *The American Church in Crisis*, David T. Olson is pretty blunt about our churches today.[8] He says, "A generation can become 'culture-bound' and not notice they are increasingly out of touch with the changes. It is always easy for a generation to see the flaws in the previous generation, yet miss their own shortcomings." This is a sobering thought. Let it serve as a wake-up call to our churches today. In order to continue to glorify God's bride, the Church, all churches must step up and regroup, rethink, retry, and search their hearts to find what God wants them to do.

In the following chapters we will look at some cultural trends. You will find research and ideas about using technology to attract people to your church. We'll discuss the varied family arrangements and lifestyles and what these families want in a church. We'll provide you with resources and ideas about improving and updating your church physically as well as offer ideas to help you bring your members onboard so they too can serve in our great calling—serving God through the local church.

Chapter 2

What Parents Want

All your sons will be taught by the LORD,
and great will be your children's peace.

—Isaiah 54:13

What do families want in a church? What do they look for when they visit your church? These seem to be the questions almost every church is asking. Families have changed dramatically in the past few years, and modern-day families come in many different shapes and forms.

The modern-day traditional families are not only concerned about their children; they also are more concerned with their children's wants and needs than ever before. Many are "helicopter parents" who hover over their children. They are savvy parents, and they will hold your church accountable for providing the most up-to-date equipment and programming. Mainly they want

- a strong children's ministry for infants through youth that will cater to the individual needs of their child,
- a safe place for their children,
- a place that meets the adult's need for spiritual growth, and
- a place where adults and children feel loved and accepted.

While I was visiting with a church leader in North Carolina about modern-day families, the leader said, "Upon coming to our church for the first time, many parents of preschool-age children will want the church to allow one if not both parents to sit on the perimeter of the room to see and watch what the teacher is doing and how their child is treated or accepted into the group. They also want to inspect the rooms, and some will expect a tour of the various classrooms."

A church pastor in Michigan, during a discussion about new visiting families, said, "'What do you have for my children?' is the first question perspective members ask me when visiting our church."

Attracting the Modern Family

Families want *and expect* a quality children's and youth ministry. Many want the children's ministry to have a person dedicated to overseeing this area of ministry. This can be a children's minister or a layperson who works under an overseeing minister. Parents want the children's person to create activities that are fun. When you ask many parents what they want for their children and youth, the first thing the majority will say is, "fun things to do." And while many won't say it out loud, they are thinking that they want their kids to be entertained. This is especially true of the parents of teens.

After wanting the kids to have fun, most parents want a ministry that creates relationships and invests in the children's spiritual growth. Parents expect the church to do *all of the spiritual teaching* of their children. These might possibly be parents that simply don't know how to train and develop their children's spiritual lives.

When I asked one minister what brings these parents into the church, his comment was, "Many parents will tell you, 'We just know it is right to let the kids grow up in church. It is the right thing to do—grow up in church.' They might not know much about church, but there is something about coming to church that they want their children to experience. They want God in the kid's life."

Another minister, Greg Baird, wrote, "Few parents or children will articulate this, but it's an expectation in most families: They want and expect a spiritual investment by the church. Yes, parents are primarily responsible for the discipleship of their children, but that does not mean the church has no responsibility in this area. This may seem obvious, but it requires an intentional approach that many ministries lack."[1]

Typical Midsize Church

When I was researching information for this chapter, I visited with a church leader in a midsize church in North Carolina. This church is a fast-growing church with a contemporary service in a family-oriented community, and most families have two working parents. This church realized very quickly that with active children involved in many after-school activities, these working parents didn't have much time to give to church, so they made their church family friendly for the kinds of families they have in their community.

This church was just getting ready to move into a new location—for their entire existence, they have not met in a church building. The church leader said one of the things several families have shared is they want to attend a church that is actually located in a church building. They will join when the church is set up in its permanent building. They don't want their families to attend a church in a school, a mall, a shopping area, or a community center. They value a church building. And most of the families who come to visit this church are typical of the modern-day parent:

- They are concerned for their children's safety.
- They will ask about safety procedures and protocols.
- They want to know if the church has completed background checks on all volunteers.
- They ask if the teachers and volunteers have received training.
- They want to know the teachers' names. They seem to feel better and more comfortable with the leaders if they know their names.

Other church leaders with young parents just starting their families say,

- "Our congregants want an attractive nursery."
- "Congregants expect nursery workers who smile, coo, and in general show love for babies."

Our church leader friend says he gives all visiting families a "ninety-second spiel" about what the kids will be doing. He gives them an idea of what the kids can expect. Included in his ninety-second talk are safety issues. He explains their drop-off and pick-up system. He also assures the parents someone will come and get them if there is a problem with their child. He says most parents want to partner with the church, and mostly they want to feel good about where they are leaving their children. He also says, "For the most part the overconcerned or helicopter parents in our church don't want to actually volunteer. However, they do want to observe often."

He goes on to explain that for some children having the parent observing or popping in and checking on them makes the child nervous. He wonders if the parents' worries actually cause the child undue stress, wondering if there is something wrong. Is the child wondering if he or she is safe or if there is a reason the parents are concerned? He thinks some kids might not feel safe simply because the parents' body language says things aren't safe. But he says, "That's what you get when you reach out to the modern-day two-parent family."

Safety Issues

When parents check out the rooms and physical space for children, they are looking for safety issues. Safety issues might mean they look for equipment that is new or in good condition. Equipment needs to meet current safety standards. Parents also look for cleanliness. Safety issues can mean they want to know what protocols and procedures are in place for

- medical emergencies,
- diaper changing,
- power outages,
- fire safety/drills,
- severe weather,
- bomb threats, and
- lockdown procedures (armed intruder).

Fire Safety

When considering your children's area for fire safety, consult with your local fire department as many states have fire codes for children's rooms and nurseries in churches. Here are a few tips and suggestions to get you started assessing your church for fire safety and also for developing a fire safety checklist.[2]

- Fire exit routes posted in every room. These instructions should be mounted and encased in unbreakable glass or plastic so they can't be removed.
- Diagram posted in every room showing the location of fire extinguishers.
- Key leaders trained in how to use fire extinguishers.
- Fire department, police, and emergency numbers along with the church's name and full address and phone number posted on the evacuation route.
- Periodic fire drills scheduled throughout the year. For weeklong programs such as Vacation Bible School, do at least one fire drill during the week so children and workers will be aware of the procedures. (Children are used to fire drills at school and childcare.)
- Each room has two means of egress. Some states allow windows to be a means of exiting a room in case of a fire. Or they will allow one door in the room to open to another inside room.

- For newer buildings or renovated areas, many fire codes require each children's room to have an exit to the outside. These doors can remain locked but must have a push bar so escape can be made quickly and easily in case of an emergency.
- Exits are clear and clutter free. You can't believe the churches I have visited where chairs, shelves, cribs, and stuff block the exit doors.
- Exit room doors open out. In other words, should there be a fire, leaders would be able to push the exit doors open instead of trying to pull inward. If leaders are worried about children trying to escape, the doorknob to the room can be located higher than children can reach.
- Window dressings as well as cloth decorations hung around the room are fire resistant or coated with a fire-resistant substance.
- Ceiling lights are covered with some type of shield. Some fire codes allow plastic tubes that cover fluorescent lights if light shields are not installed.
- Electrical outlets have plugs covering each outlet.

Intruder Prevention

It is sad to think we have to worry about protecting our children at church, but there have been cases when an armed person or a shooter has walked into a church building with the intent to do harm. Since there have been several school shootings—and who can forget the Sandy Hook Elementary School in Newtown, Connecticut, where kindergartners were killed—parents have become concerned about church safety.

Many parents are now used to school lockdowns and security personnel at their children's school. They also expect churches to provide the same type of safety measures when it comes to their children's safety at church. Churches might want to consult their local schools and follow some of the same procedures. Or bring in a specialist or a local police chief to evaluate the facility.

Here are some suggestions for developing your own policies, procedures, and safety check list:

- Written policies and procedures regarding intruder prevention are made available to all volunteers and church leaders, including those who are not in the children's rooms.
- All church leaders and children's volunteers are trained in what to do in case a shooter should enter the facility or shots are heard around the building.
- Training is available in person, in written form, or on video.
- All doors to children's rooms can be locked from the inside in case a lockdown has to take place.
- Emergency numbers are posted and a phone is available at all times.
- A code, alarm, or some means of notifying volunteers and children's leaders of a lockdown is in place. Some churches use the fire alarm but use short blasts instead of one long sound.
- A designated meeting place away from the church is readily available in case children need to evacuate the facility.
- A system is in place to make sure parents are aware of this location.
- A list of all children in attendance in the room where the children are located is made available and kept up-to-date. If groups of children rotate to other rooms, the attendance list should accompany the children to the new location. The list should include cell phone or emergency numbers where a parent can be reached in case of evacuation to another location. This is particularly true in programs such as Vacation Bible School when the parents are not on the property. (This is also a good idea in case of a fire evacuation.)

- Designated volunteers, an off-duty police officer, or a sheriff are assigned to walk around the perimeter of the church building during services.
- A system is in place for access to the children's area. Only allow parents of children in attendance at the time to enter the children's area.
- All outside doors are locked from the outside. Make sure the doors can be opened from the inside at all times.

Upon going into a lockdown mode

- lock all inside doors and windows,
- take roll immediately,
- notify 9-1-1 and give the address of your church,
- isolate the children and keep them out of sight,
- keep children as quiet as possible, and
- cover windows in doors or other means of looking into a room.

Other Safety Issues

Other issues include a drop-off and pick-up system, a method for checking children in upon arrival, and a check-out system. Kid-Check suggests, "Have clearly defined drop-off and pick-up times and location. These should be clearly communicated and enforced. The children of volunteers should remain with their parents or be supervised in one location. Do not allow early drop-offs when volunteers are not present."[3]

There are many systems for checking children in and out. Today's computer-based systems are secure, affordable, and efficient. It is imperative that you establish some sort of check-in and check-out system. Whether you have an up-to-date computer system or an old-fashioned pencil-and-paper or number system, have something in place so parents will feel safe leaving their children with you.

Background Screening

Use criminal background checks to protect your church. As of the writing of this book, no court has found a church liable for child sexual abuse based on a claim of negligence on account of the church's failure to perform a criminal background check on a molester. According to the people that produce the Reducing the Risk DVD series, it is worth noting that a growing number of churches and youth-serving organizations are performing criminal records checks on volunteers, and this suggests that the court one day may conclude that "reasonable care" in the selection of children's/youth volunteers necessitates a criminal background check. Therefore, churches that conduct criminal records checks on volunteers who work with minors will be in a better position—both now and in the future—to defend against allegations of negligent selection.[4]

Always make sure you have

- criminal background checks on all paid and volunteer staff—this is crucial if you want to have a safe children's ministry—and
- at least two adults present at all times.

Teacher Training

Most parents want to know your volunteers have received some type of training in church protocols and safety precautions. They want to know three things:

- Do teachers understand basic first aid?
- Do leaders know how to handle discipline situations?
- Do teachers know how to teach age-appropriate materials?

Children's Spaces

Parents look for attractive rooms that are designed for children, with colors, shapes, and characters that appeal to children. They want up-to-date environments. The beige walls and unattractive decorations that have been hanging around from two decades ago are not going to attract the modern-day parent. Grandma Helen's crochet wall hanging that was made in the 1960s might have to go the way of the 1960s.

Parents are used to contemporary prefabricated environments. They spend enormous amounts on their children's rooms at home, and they want churches to create the same kind of attractive and inviting environment.

Some churches bring in experts who paint elaborate scenes on their church walls. While I don't think this is necessary, some thought and planning must go into the design of your décor and the overall look.

If you use neutral colors on walls and floors, decorate with posters or decorate based on the curriculum or a particular theme. Matt McKee, a pastor of students and children at Horizon Community Church in Cincinnati, Ohio, says, "I bought a HP5500 42-inch plotter [a large-format printer]. I print off all of my own sets, backdrops, signs, and props, which change every six to eight weeks and I print off a new environment for our children's space at least twice a year."[5]

Keeping clutter to a minimum also helps entice parents. Every leader needs to take a critical look at her or his children's rooms. Assess what needs to go, or perhaps what needs to be purchased, in order to keep things looking neat, clean, and orderly.

Curriculum

Many modern parents are inquisitive when it comes to children's curriculum. They are likely to ask questions about what their children are learning and what curriculum your church is using. When considering what curriculum to use for your children's ministry, DiscipleBlog.com has some great ideas about evaluating curriculum.

An evaluation of curriculum for your children's ministry should follow these ten foci:

1. Bible Literacy

Does the curriculum encourage children to use their own Bibles?

2. Relational bonding

Does the curriculum encourage healthy intergenerational and peer relationships?

3. Global perspective

Does the curriculum provide opportunities to learn what God is doing around the world?

4. Teacher friendly

Do the Teacher Guides provide easy-to-follow lesson plans with creative activity ideas?

5. Life-change

Does the curriculum encourage genuine life transformation opportunities?

6. Church compatibility

Does the curriculum dovetail with your church's core values and overall direction?

7. Scope & sequence

Does the curriculum follow a clear plan that ensures your children will receive balanced spiritual growth?

8. Culturally relevant

Does the curriculum speak to "where children are" in life?

9. Developmentally appropriate

Does the curriculum provide clear learning objectives for each lesson?

10. Church + home

Does the curriculum suggest practical ways parents can become involved in spiritual growth?[6]

Protecting Marriages

Married couples look for marriage-enrichment classes. With all the societal issues affecting two-parent families in our communities, couples want and need help.

Elizabeth Marquardt, who has done extensive research on marriage and divorce, says,

> Marriage is not merely a private arrangement; it is also a complex social institution. Marriage helps to unite the needs and desires of couples and the children their unions produce. Because marriage fosters small cooperative unions—otherwise known as stable families—it not only enables children to thrive, but also shores up communities, helping family members to succeed during good times and to weather the bad times.[7]

In order to bring two-parent families into the church, pastors and elders might want to rethink their roles in this responsibility to the families in their communities. Part of the concern is to understand the fact that two-parent middle-class marriages are slowly morphing into marriages of the upper class or more educated people. Katelyn Beaty, managing editor of *Christianity Today*, reports on the Family Scholars site, "Once the icon of solid marriages and two-parent families, the middle class is starting to resemble the poor's relationship patterns: cohabitation, serial partnerships, divorce, and single parenting aided by welfare."[8]

In *The State of Our Unions* published by the National Marriage Project at the University of Virginia and the Institute for American Values' Center for Marriage and Families, we learn the following:

> We are also witnessing a striking exodus from marriage, especially among high school but not college educated young people, for whom raising children amid unstable cohabiting relationships and serial partnerships is in danger of becoming the new norm. This rapid decline of marriage among the almost 60 percent of the nation who are high school educated but not college educated, those whom we might call "Middle America," has been dramatic. As recently as the 1980s, only 13 percent of the children of moderately educated mothers were born outside of marriage. By the late 2000s, this figure rose to a striking 44 percent. And in marked contrast to past calls for attention to changing trends in family structure, today almost none of our political and social leaders are talking about this dramatic change.[9]

And I might add, neither is the religious sector.

Since the 1970s, marriages have taken a hit. While there aren't as many divorces today, as the report above states, there are more couples cohabitating. Living together before marriage seems to be the stipulation for many couples. Many of the couples today have at least one partner that experienced the divorce of their own family. They don't want to make the same mistake as their parents. However, they have not had many models in their lives to emulate. "'You mean it is wrong to live together before marriage?' is the question we hear from cohabitating couples that attend our church. "These young couples simply do not understand biblical concepts," said one pastor in Michigan.

Has your church thought about how you will handle a situation where a cohabitating couple with children wants to join your church family?

- Will you turn them away?
- Will you accept them and gently expose them to your church's beliefs?

- Will you, when they are ready, encourage them to marry?

There are no easy answers, but study and pray about these issues so that you will be prepared to deal with them. I promise you, if you are reaching out to your community, this will become an issue.

What Churches Can Do

- Presenting sermons on what the Bible says about marriages is the first step. Make these sermons family friendly for all kinds of families, including single-parent and blended families.
- Host marriage enrichment weekends. Do this more than once a year. Or make it an annual event so couples can learn to depend on the uplifting weekend.
- Present a small-group series on marriage that meets weekly.
- Celebrate long-term marriages.
- Host seminars or courses about what happens when a couple divorces. Many people jump into a divorce without actually thinking through all of the ramifications of what divorce does to the children. Programs such as "Choosing Wisely" will help couples understand the many issues that accompany a divorce.[10]
- Pair up couples who indicate their marriage is on the rocks with strong biblical couples who will mentor them.
- Host classes on budgeting and finances.

Three Things Modern-Day Parents Wish Churches Would Consider

Greg Baird says parents want the following:

- "Flexibility. Families are busier than ever. While I don't necessarily like it, families don't want or need the expectation of weekly attendance or presence at every church event. Truth is, most churches have ridiculous expectations of families when the entire calendar is combined."

- "Excellence. . . . I believe excellence means high standards in how we present our program and variety in what program we present."
- "Communication. Maybe I should say 'constant' communication. . . . Making our communication stand out, offered through a variety of channels, and making it consistent, is necessary and expected by families." [11]

Top 10 Things Modern-Day Parents Look for in a Church

1. A place that is safe and has safe people

2. A church where programming is coordinated and of quality

3. A facility that is attractive and has organized children's rooms

4. An environment where teachers have been trained

5. A church that has unconditional love for children and where there are no judgments about how parents are raising their children

6. A church that provides biblical principles of parenting to help its members parent in today's world

7. Nurseries that will make sure babies have dry diapers and are fed on schedule

8. Children's programs that teach children spiritual lessons (they don't want babysitting)

9. A place where they can find mentorship programs for troubled youth

10. A church that teaches the gospel and biblical
    principles

When I was researching this chapter, I put a note on my Face-book page asking people what they thought modern-day families were looking for in a church. Following are just a few of the typical responses. I pray you will learn as much from their answers as I did.

Person 1: "Less shows and productions and more from the word of God!"

Person 2: "A happy face from church workers and members . . . because sometimes it's the only one you may see."

Person 3: "I think having a church family that reaches out. One that holds activities for the whole family to be in-volved in and encourages its members. When you feel part of something, you want to stay part of it. Sure, we all want to hear the word of God and the message from each sermon. But being part of more than that brings you closer and keeps you wanting more from the church you attend. Also having church members that reach out and really show others the love of God. At least that is my take on it."

Person 4: "One that's led by the Holy Spirit."

Person 5: "I think with the explosion of technology that we are losing the human touch. We don't notice when people don't show up nor act like we care. I know this is not the only reason to be at church but it makes a huge impact!!!"

Person 6: "I want a place where we can all feel connected with the services of the church. My son likes to ask questions . . . lots of questions. An environment of sit-and-listen is not conducive to him. Just because he's eight doesn't mean he doesn't want to serve. He wants the opportunity sing in church, lead prayer, and ask questions like the rest of us. His father and I like a place that he is allowed to grow in the Spirit and not feel confined."

Person 7: "Been thinking further on this. I believe the question should be, What do modern-day families need in a church? What do leaders need to do to bring them to the place where they will want what they need? In studying the Old Testament we see that when the leaders were strong the people were strong; when the leaders were weak the people were weak."

Person 8: "I still believe that a church must be a part of the community, not just be there for the congregation. Charity is where you begin to grow your family. It does not matter how big or small the task might be, a community sees what you're trying to accomplish and more will come because they see the good."

Person 9: "Trust in leadership; a congregation that loves and prays and really gets to know the needs of the people. Church shouldn't be a social club for those who have been there a long time while newer members (or attendees) are left to continue to almost be strangers and to deal with our needs by ourselves. If we truly believe that church is a gathering place of sinners who are making efforts to become more like Jesus (rather than a place where only perfect, pious people come to feel even better about themselves), then we all have an obligation to help each other. That responsibility is ours, but must start at the top with strong and COMPASSIONATE leadership."

Person 10: "Sad to say but a large part of what they want is entertainment! They also want good loving care for their young children."

Person 11: "We changed to a different denomination about four years ago. Just the other night at a choir party, we discussed just this thing. What seemed to be expressed the most was the fact our church welcomes all, no judging. I have never felt so at home in a church. It is not unusual to see homeless people wander in, and they are welcomed with open arms."

Person 12: "Unconditional Love. Resources. Mentorship."

Person 13: "Biblical teachings, servant's attitude, harmony among church family and active members would be four on the top of my list."

Person 14: "Church family and unity in worship."

Person 15: "A place to be connected spiritually and physically. A place where I feel wanted and/or useful by being invited to volunteer."

Chapter 3

Taking a Page out of the Book of Nehemiah

For whoever does the will of my Father in heaven
is my brother and sister and mother.

—Matthew 12:50

As I began to think about attracting nontraditional families, I thought about all the varied family types in the Bible. In fact, in the Bible, I can't find a single two-parent traditional family that lives on a corner lot in the suburbs. I realize some of you may scoff at that statement, and yet when you talk to nontraditional families, they will tell you they don't feel accepted in many churches simply because they don't fit the typical, traditional, two-parent mold. Diana Garland, dean of Baylor School of Social Work, helped design the Church Census.[1] She says the Church Census defines families as those who act like a family to one another, whether or not those roles match up with the traditional nuclear family.[2]

Some nontraditional families need churches to reach out and minister to them in order to attract them to the church. Other nontraditional families just need an invitation to come to your church. Many people are waiting to be invited or accepted into the church family. Here is a story I've heard repeated many times: Carmella,[3] who was from another country, was a widow with an elementary-age son. After her husband died she felt alone and yearned for family. She found "family" in a single-parent group. The single-parent small-group Bible study wasn't in her church or her denomination, but it was a group that felt like family.

The following scripture is how my friend Carmella felt when she found the church that had a single-parent group: "He replied, 'My mother and brothers are those who hear God's word and put it into practice'" (Luke 8:21).

When I was praying about how to challenge ministers to reach out to various family structures, Nehemiah came to my mind. I saw how Nehemiah's story could serve as an analogy for churches today. If you remember, Nehemiah was distressed that the gates of Jerusalem were in need of repair. "Those who survived the exile and are back in the province are in great trouble and disgrace. The wall of Jerusalem is broken down, and its gates have been burned with fire" (Nehemiah 1:3). The people had made it through the exile, but they were troubled. They had no protection because the walls of Jerusalem were broken and destroyed.

In the second chapter of Nehemiah we find Nehemiah going before the king, and the king says to him, "Why does your face look so sad when you are not ill? This can be nothing but sadness of heart" (v. 2). Nehemiah explained that his face looked sad and his heart was troubled because the city where his fathers were buried lay in ruins. He wanted to go and repair the gates and the walls surrounding the city so the people would be protected.

Today the walls and the gates to our society lie in ruins. Our society and especially our children are not protected, and our society as we know it may cease to exist if we don't start repairing the walls and the gates of our families. Our Lord's face must be sad because of what our society is doing and the sin in our world. Nehemiah knew the hope for Jerusalem lay in repairing the walls and gates. It might be prudent to follow Nehemiah's example and apply his tactics in our churches today.

What if we began to look at the families in our communities as our walls and gates? We can follow Nehemiah's plan for how he got started. "When I heard these things, I sat down and wept. For some days I mourned and fasted and prayed before the God of heaven"

(1:4). The families in your community need for you to weep, mourn, fast, and pray for the Lord's direction. Not every church is going to be able to reach every kind of family structure, but each church can get started seeking the Lord's direction. Ask God what kind of families your church needs to reach. Employ God to guide and direct your church.

Nehemiah had a plan for his day. He and the leaders sprang up to replace the gates. "They laid its beams and put its door and bolts and bars in place" (3:3). In other words, they got started. How is your church rebuilding the foundations and making families feel safe today? What beams and bolts are you putting in place to accommodate the families in your community?

The leaders in Nehemiah's story reached out to the walls and gates in front of them, behind them, and across from them. Others tried to stop them. And at times they had to build with one hand while they held their weapons with the other hand. Today the families that are in our churches are going to have to reach out to the nontraditional families to the right, to the left, and across the street from them. This means including the following types of families:

- Single-parent families
- Blended families
- Grandparents parenting again
- Boomerang children and their families
- Adult children of divorce and their families
- Single adults in the church today (the church becomes their family)
- Boomers
- Cohabitation families
- The children with three legal parents

In next few chapters you will be given some particulars about various nontraditional families that will hopefully inspire your church to enhance your ministry and reach new families.

At this point you may be saying to yourself

- "There is no way I can add anything else to my plate."
- "We are a small church and I don't have the personnel to expand."
- "My staff is spread too thin now."
- "We already have too many hurting families in our church."
- "We don't have the money to make a lot of improvements, even though we know we need them."
- "I'm not a counselor; how can I minister to all these different kinds of families?"

The good news is you don't have to do this alone. There are many other people and situations that can help you:

- For many of these families, they will come to your church when a friend invites them.
- They will come when they can connect with someone who has had a similar experience.
- They will come when they know someone in the church will empathize with their situation. For many of these situations it will not be the head or senior pastor or the paid church staff but the people who sit in the pews of your church.
- They will come when they can tell their stories.
- They will come when presented with God's truths.
- They will keep coming when, with gentleness and care, the gospel is applied to the sin in their lives.
- They will keep coming when they feel loved by you and by the church and they are convinced God loves them so much that he sent his son to die on the cross for their sins.
- They will continue to attend when they can contribute and are encouraged to serve.

Learn the stories of the people already in your congregation. I've helped start DivorceCare, DivorceCare for Kids, and GriefShare at churches around the country. In almost every church, couples come up to me and, very quietly, almost secretively, say something like, "You may not know this, but we are in our second marriage. We each were divorced years ago (or widowed) and then we found each other and married. Not many people in our church know this."

This tells me pastors and church leaders may not know the stories of the people in their congregations. So think about conducting a demographic study of the people in your church. You could make up your own that could be simple and straightforward. You could also use a professional one like the Church Census.[4] The Church Census was developed by Baylor Center for Family and Community Ministries. It is a tool developed for assessing your congregational family life. It will help you to get to know the families in your congregation. Something else the Church Census discovered is that even though families are struggling, they still want to serve others.

There might be several people in your own church who have survived a crisis or trauma and they are ready to serve if only asked to so do. Please allow them to comfort others.

Here are some ideas from Mike McManus, cofounder and cochair of Marriage Savers:

- Restoration: Troubled marriages can be restored by training couples whose own marriages once nearly failed, to mentor those in crisis, saving four out of five troubled marriages.
- Stepfamily Support Group: Stepfamilies divorce at a 70 percent rate, but a support group, where couples with stepchildren meet regularly, could save 80 percent of them.[5]

Allow the people in your congregation the opportunity to share their stories and live out 2 Corinthians 1:3-5: "Praise be to the God and Father of our Lord Jesus Christ, the Father of compassion and the God of all comfort, who comforts us in all our troubles, so that we can comfort those in any trouble with the comfort we ourselves receive from God. For just as we share abundantly in the sufferings of Christ, so also our comfort abounds through Christ."

It's about Understanding

Like I said in the first chapter, getting these families into your church is not about programs or gimmicks:

- It is about understanding each family type.
- It is about understanding how their families operate.
- It is about connecting with them.
- It is about relationships.

You are probably thinking to yourself, "Okay, she has said this about relationships about a dozen times by now. I get it!" I am convinced that the people in our communities are starving for relationships, so be prepared, because I will keep saying it. If we can't form relationships with them, how can we expect them to form a relationship with God and accept Christ as their Savior when we are his representation?

Other Family Structures

There are myriad family structures in our world today. Although each of these various family structures needs an entire chapter of its own, we are only going to take a brief look at some of them. I'm not saying you need to label these various family structures, but knowing their makeups and particular needs will help create the church spoken about in the New Testament. All of these families need the gospel. They need to know biblical truths and precepts.

On the Family Ministry Church Leader's Facebook page I asked the question, "What do all of you think would bring nontraditional families into the local churches today? What do these families want in a church?" Here is a wonderful post in reply:

> The gospel. Let us (the church) never move from what people need to what they want. If we have the gospel, we have everything.
>
> What will make them feel welcome? The gospel.

What will make them feel loved? The gospel.

What will change the way they parent? The gospel.

What will restore broken & hurting relationships (past, present, future)? The gospel.

What will transform their thinking, life, home, workplace, and city? The gospel.

I know this sounds like a petty answer, but it is true. When the gospel becomes real in the church, the world will be drawn to it. Legalism and moralism will fall away and the finished work of Christ will be magnified.

Everywhere Jesus went droves of sinners followed—why? He brought the gospel to them.[6]

How Do We Reach Out?

How do we reach people and bring the gospel to them and their families? The people in the pews are the ones who can do this. They need to reach out wherever they encounter these people—at the grocery store, the mall, the neighborhood get-together, school, and so on. We need to send someone to them instead of expecting people to show up at our churches asking to be included in ministry. Can you only imagine if each intact family in your church reached out and impacted one family in your community? Church people could change the world just like the disciples did in the New Testament.

Rolesville Baptist Church in Rolesville, North Carolina, does an incredible job of reaching out to the community through their Operation Inasmuch ministry.[7] Operation Inasmuch is based on Matthew 25:40: "The King will reply, 'Truly I tell you, whatever you did for one of the least of these brothers and sisters of mine, you did for me.'" One Saturday every spring the church comes together for Operation Inasmuch. Before that Saturday arrives hundreds of man-hours have been spent collecting furniture, linens, baby clothes, food, money, lumber, plants, flowers, and anything you can think of that a family in their community might need. Other church members scout the community, finding families who might need help. They work with the schools in the area to help identify families in need. Teams are formed weeks in advance of Operation Inasmuch as church members sign up for their area of expertise. Even teens and children sign up for a team.

On the morning of Operation Inasmuch, the church family gathers early for a hardy breakfast. Teams then meet in the gym, where assignments are handed out to the team leader. Before blast off, everyone joins in prayer for the service and the witnessing that is going to take place. The list of what this one church has done is endless, but here are a few examples:

- Repaired an older widow's home.
- Built a ramp for an older man in a wheelchair.
- Built a ramp for a trailer where a child in a wheelchair lived.
- Cut down falling trees, mowed, and landscaped one family's yard.
- Chopped wood for a single mom who heats her house with wood.
- Delivered specified sizes of children's clothes to a widow who didn't have the funds to clothe her three children. Food and paper items were also delivered.
- Hosted a backyard VBS for kids at the trailer park while furniture, linens, bedding, paper goods, and food were delivered to families in trailers. The kids were introduced to Jesus and to loving people. A lunch was served to all the kids, and when some of them returned to their homes, they had a bed to sleep in, clean sheets, age-appropriate toys, and books to read.

Although Operation Inasmuch doesn't bring people into the church the next Sunday, it does create loving relationships with those in the community. People talk and neighbors share about what "that church" is doing in the community.

One year after our Saturday with Operation Inasmuch, a struggling single mom shared with me that she turned to the church to meet a need in her life. She said before she was too embarrassed, but after seeing the church working so hard in the community, she felt comfortable enough to know that she wouldn't be judged or criticized by the church people.

The other thing that Operation Inasmuch does is tighten bonds within the church family. People get to know one another. They visit, laugh, and connect while they are doing something worthwhile in the community. People who normally wouldn't donate time or serve in another capacity will show up for Operation Inasmuch. Create community bonds within the church and that will flow out into the community surrounding your church.

Ministries Become Intertwined

You may already have a ministry to the older population, and some of them may already be acting as full-time caregivers to their grandchildren. Why not ask someone in the group who is not caring for grandchildren to research grandparents parenting again? By recruiting some of the grandparents and some singles in your church, you could start a grandparent care ministry through which you give the grandparents caring for grandchildren some respite days.

Adult children of divorce who have healed and are spiritually mature and emotionally healthy could mentor children from single-parent families who have no access to the other parent.

The ideas for ministry are limitless when you tap into the servants already in your congregation. Make your church a launchpad into the community. Being relational but also relevant, intentional, and creative will bring in many nontraditional families. I pray the Lord will open your eyes to reach out and look for these families in your church and in your community.

Chapter 4

Creating a Family-Friendly Church for Single-Parent Families

God sets the lonely in families.

—Psalm 68:6

Jena stood in the middle of the hallway unsure of which way to go.[1] She couldn't find her way back to her children. She had gone to a Bible study class after a nice lady had helped her take her children to the children's wing, but where was that? All the people in her class had disappeared. She began to sob quietly as panic set in.

Rosa was a single mom, and she had come to this church because she had heard they had something for single parents.[2] She had visited many churches since her husband had been killed serving his country overseas. After his death she had to move out of base housing. Since he was killed right after he had moved her to this area, she hadn't had an opportunity to make friends. She had hoped that this church might allow her to find a place where she and her children would fit in and where she would not be looked upon as a poor, pitiful young widow. The pastor called her later in the week and told her they had no place for her at his church because, "After all, our widows are senior citizens. What would we do with you and your young children?"

Chuck was a single dad of a ten-year-old girl and an eight-year-old boy.[3] The children's choir was singing at church that night. His daughter was in tears because he couldn't figure out how to put her hair into some kind of special braid. He stood in the church foyer as his tearful daughter walked to the choir room. He had been coming to this church for several months now but knew no one. The divorce had devastated him; he could barely keep his wits about him, and now his daughter was crying. He had never felt so alone in his entire life as he did at this very moment.

If you've never walked in the shoes of a single parent, you might think Jena, Rose, and Chuck are being oversensitive. But I can tell you from my own personal experience that the feelings of our three friends are very real.

There is more to creating a family-friendly church for single parents than programs:

- Single parents need relationships. Relationships are the key in bringing and keeping single parents in the church—relationships with people in the church and with Christ.
- They want to be able to contribute to the church family.
- They need understanding of their situation.
- They need acceptance.
- They need to be validated as worthwhile Christians.
- They need encouragement.
- They need people who will help teach their children biblical truths and model strong Christian marriages.
- They need for the church family to realize that they are parenting alone and that is different from parenting with a spouse.

Developing and adapting the heart toward single-parent families is crucial if you want them to enter the doors of your church. It means accepting all single parents who come to your church. It means using gentleness in applying biblical standards to those who are hurting or those living a sinful lifestyle. It means adapting the church's physical environment as well as understanding the stages of single parenting.

There are several reasons people are parenting alone. They include the following:

- Death of a spouse
- Divorce
- Separation of cohabitating partners
- Never married
- Adoption
- Incarceration of a spouse
- Mental illness
- Desertion by a spouse

The number of single parents continues to increase in our society. The statistics for children being raised in single-parent families is staggering. Nationwide, the average percentage of single parents raising children is 35 percent.[4] Some states, such as Mississippi, run as high as 47 percent, with Louisiana coming in at 45 percent. For many years now, over one million children a year experience the divorce of their parents. According to a report released in November 2009 by the U.S. Census Bureau and reported by About.com Single Parents section,

- 21.8 million children under the age of 21 are being raised by a single parent,
- 82.6 percent are mothers,
- 17.4 percent are fathers, and
- 24.6 percent earn less than the federal poverty level.[5]

If you want to find out what the percentage of children living in single-parent households, living with cohabitating domestic partners, and other household types is for your state, check out the Annie E. Casey Foundation's Kids Count site.[6] The Annie E. Casey Foundation will also convert the percentage to the actual number of children. In addition, they break these numbers down to congressional districts and, for some states, to cities.

In the congressional district where I live in Florida, forty-six thousand children live in mother-only households and ten thousand children in father-only households. This means tonight fifty-six thousand children in the small panhandle area of Florida will go to bed in a single-parent household. And the majority of those children will not attend a church on a regular basis. Some will never attend church. That is a huge number of children who will have no exposure to God or Christ and may never enter the Kingdom.

The church must step up and realize how important it is to minister to the ever-growing population of single parents and their children. Research shows most divorced single parents drop out of church. Jennifer Maggio, who runs a dynamic single-moms program at Healing Place Church in Baton Rouge, Louisiana, says, "We hear that nearly 70% of single mothers in our country do not actively attend church (many citing fear and shame as reasons)."[7]

Churches in the 1990s and in the first part of this century created all kinds of single-parent ministry programs. While they were well meaning, they didn't bring single parents into the church family. They brought single parents to the church building but did not integrate them into the church. Here are some examples of single-parent ministry programs:

- Car care: Churches set up Saturday sessions where single moms can bring in their cars for oil changes and other light maintenance.
- Food pantries: Local congregations provide a well-stocked food pantry so that when single parents need help feeding their children, they can come to the church and stock up on basic items.
- Clothes closet: Many churches collect all sizes of clothes and host a clothes closet one Saturday a month. Moms and dads can exchange children's clothes for another size or find needed seasonal items.

- Medical clinic: A few churches set up medical clinics where doctors and nurses volunteer their services to help single parents in their community. Single parents can bring in their sick children and receive coupons for free medications.
- Dental clinic: Churches set up dental clinics where single parents can receive free dental needs for their children or themselves.
- Dress for success: Churches collect gently used business clothes. When a single parent, usually a single mom, has to reenter the job market, she is offered help selecting a small wardrobe that will help her feel better about herself and help her look professional. She is given two or three nice outfits.
- Job help: Some churches mentor single moms who have never had to work outside the home and help them learn how to write a résumé, apply for a job, and enter the workforce.
- Parenting classes: Single-parent experts are brought in for special seminars about how to parent children when parenting alone.
- Handyman available: One church I know has a crew of handymen. These men are available to help people move, fix small appliances, and repair things in the home.

Churches that run these types of ministry programs make a big mistake if they don't use the programs as an introduction to the church. One church in Florida that runs a dental clinic for a week every year has extra church volunteers available to sit with the clients. They talk with them, pray with them, and when appropriate suggest different church classes that meet various needs, such as a women's Bible study, divorce recovery program, and other classes.

You may be in a church that is not going to create a single-mom or single-dad ministry, or even a single-parent family ministry. You may not have the finances or personnel to create a separate ministry for single parents. And not every church needs to create separate classes for single parents. Jennifer Maggio's single-mom ministry only meets every other Friday and she and her team are ministering to hundreds of single moms in their area.

One word of caution: single parents do not belong in the singles ministry. Single parents have a different agenda in that they are raising children.

Hidden Mission Field

Theresa McKenna, in her book *The Hidden Mission Field: Caring for Single Parent Families in the 21st Century,* says that the hidden mission field is the families in the apartment complexes down the street from your church.[8] If we don't step up and minister to these children and bring them into the church and if we don't change our mind-set about ministering to these families, we may see numbers dwindling in churches in the future.

The following information was given by the Heritage Foundation in testimony before the U.S. Senate in May of 2004:

> When parents reject each other by divorce or an out-of-wedlock birth that eventually ends in totally separate lives for the father and mother, the strengths of their children are not as developed as they could be, and more weaknesses occur in major outcomes such as deprivations, addictions, abuse, and failure.
>
> In 1950 for every hundred children born, that year, 12 entered a broken family. . . . By the year 2000 that number had risen five-fold and for every 100 children born 60 entered a broken family.[9]

Essentially in fifty years in our society, many children went from being a part of a culture of *belonging* to being part of a culture of *rejection*. Sadly, most of these children haven't been accepted in the church family either. Many adult children of divorce will tell you that the rejection of their church hurt almost as much as the divorce itself.

Research from several sources shows that children who do not live in two-parent families are more likely to engage in or suffer from the following:

- Suicide as teens. We now have children younger than twelve years of age attempting and completing suicide.[10]
- Crime, alcohol, and drug abuse.
- Behavioral problems. Even preschool-age children are exhibiting unruly and disruptive behaviors.
- Sexual activity. Some reports show that children as young as ten years of age are engaging in some form of sexual behavior.
- Abuse.
- Health problems.
- Poor performance in math. Take-away problems are too close to what has happened at home.[11] Or addition problems may remind them of the addition of stepsiblings in one of their families.
- Poor performance in reading and spelling.
- Repetition of a grade or drop out of high school.
- Divorced parents who move into the poverty level.
- A reduction in religious worship after the divorce of their parents.

Young adults in particular face staggering consequences:

- Only 42 percent of fourteen- to eighteen-year-olds live in a first-marriage birth family.[12]
- At least 25 percent of adults between eighteen and thirty-five experienced their parents' divorce.[13]
- Much of the young adult population has a disdain for organized religion.

Many of our states forget the children when it comes to supporting marriage initiatives to lower the divorce rate. I used to say, "If we don't work with the children, then in a few years when our churches are getting complacent about divorce, I fear we are going to see the divorce rate escalate." I was wrong, because now many couples don't bother to marry but rather cohabitate. Could this phenomenon be because churches didn't step up and minister to the hundreds of children of divorce from the past few generations?

Single-parent families caused by divorce can become self-perpetuating. Since the 1970s, over a million children a year have experienced the divorce of their parents. And unless there is some intervention, these children will more than likely end up divorcing when they marry or never marrying and end up cohabitating several times. They may never marry. Only by building up our families and seriously ministering to single-parent families can we end this vicious cycle.

Three Stages Single Parents Go Through

As I have observed and worked with single parents, I've come to the conclusion that most single parents go through three distinct stages.[14] There is no time limit on these stages. For some people it might be six years, others six months, and for some it might be sixteen years.

1. Survivor Stage or Crisis Stage: Barely Able to Function

This is the newly divorced or families that have experienced a death or desertion. They may find they need financial assistance or other assistance during this stage (housing, counseling, food, transportation, help help help!). DivorceCare[15] or GriefShare[16] or other "help" type ministries are needed at this stage.

This is when the child needs group support programs such DC4K that are designed specifically for the child.[17]

This, unfortunately, is the only stage many ministers see. Pastors often feel they can't finance these people or they don't have the experience or personnel to sustain single parents long term. When single parents heal and move through these stages, they will be the most dedicated of any church members. They will give of their time, their talents/gifts, and their money. In my experience, when there is support and help, single parents move through these stages and adjust at a faster rate.

2. The Transitioning Stage: Moving from Crisis to Reality

Single parents have experienced a trauma, but life continues to move forward. They may need seminars on how to parent alone, behavior and guidance, how to handle finances, career counseling, and other things.

Walk alongside these people. The person could be the widow who has lost her husband and her insurance money has run out. She needs you and she needs help. Churches that walk alongside single parents give them support so that they are not alone. Single parents can begin to feel a part of the overall church family.

3. The Emerging Single Parent: Emerging from the Fog That Has Surrounded Them

These single parents have processed the grief and are healing from the devastation. They may find they are more interested in more in-depth Bible studies. They may be ready to contribute their talents, hobbies, and interests to the church. You find they are ready to help others that are hurting and give back to God what he has given them. They have a heartfelt understanding of 2 Corinthians 1:3-4: "Praise be to the God and Father of our Lord Jesus Christ, the Father of compassion and the God of all comfort, who comforts us in all our troubles, so that we can comfort those in any trouble with the comfort we ourselves receive from God."

This is the stage where single parents want and yearn to know more about God and his holy word. When I was back in the survivor stage, I wanted to know God more, but I was so tired all the time. I would get up early to read my Bible and I would fall asleep. I felt bad about this for years, until I read the book by Trisha McCary Rhodes called *The Soul at Rest*.[18] In this book she explains that when we are very tired God can lull us to sleep. While that was comforting, I still couldn't shake the feeling that I had disappointed God when I slept instead of reading his word.

When I was talking to Trish's mother, Betty McCary, about how I felt about sleeping through my quiet time, she told me, "What better place to sleep than in God's arms?" What this one loving woman of God said to me relieved me greatly. When I got to the emerging single-parent stage, my life had settled down, my kids were grown, and I had more time to spend in his word.

Understanding these three stages will help you as you work with and minister to single parents. Knowing the three stages will assist you so you can determine what they need. For example, if it's 11:00 p.m. on a Saturday night and your phone rings and the caller ID tells you it is a single parent you know is in the crisis stage—take a deep breath and thank God he or she is calling you.

God never designed us as human beings to parent alone. That was not his design in the first book of the Bible, nor is it today. He created a man and woman to raise children. It is not a normal or natural design to parent alone.

The Creation of the Family by God

It was God's design for people to live in families. One parent and a child are a family, but many children from single-parent homes don't feel like they live in a family. I have had children say this to me many times; "You know, I don't have a family anymore."

The first Easter alone for my children and me:

The first year my children and I were alone I had an opportunity that burned into my mind the importance of calling ourselves a family unit. It was on an Easter Sunday morning, and when we went to church that morning there was a member of the congregation taking pictures of all the families. As we approached the church, he motioned for us to come over and get our picture made. I became upset at the audacity of this man. How dare he want to take a picture of my children and me? Hadn't he heard that their father and I were divorced?

He was insistent; then I heard my daughter shout, "We don't have a family," and she went running into the church. My son was quieter, but his words were just as lethal when he said to the man, "We aren't a family anymore. Don't you know my Dad left?" With his head down and his shoulders slumped, he walked off in the opposite direction and into the church.

Oh my goodness, my children just verbalized what I had been thinking, but hearing them say it hurt. After praying all day about this, I realized my children were only replicating what I was projecting. We did have a family; it was just a different family now, and before I lost my kids to the world, I had to pull things together.

Why Do Kids Join Gangs and Not God's Family, the Church?

When families are dysfunctional and teens feel they don't belong, they will create their own families—or gangs. They join gangs because we are born to connect and belong. The desire to belong is innate. For the most part, gangs replace the disappointment kids feel when their families aren't there for them. You may ask why these kids don't turn to the church youth group. They don't turn to the church youth group because they feel different and they don't feel accepted.

Building Foundations for Families Today

Here's why we have to support single parents—because they are raising a large majority of the next generation. If we don't help, America will continue its downward spiral into social decay. Various research sources all note the following:

- divorce impedes learning by disrupting productive study patterns, as children are forced to move between homes;
- divorce diminishes children's capacity to handle conflict; and
- the drop-off in worship has serious consequences for our children.

Religion has been found to have beneficial effects on

- physical and mental health,
- education level,
- income,
- virginity in teens,
- crime addiction, and
- general happiness.

Church attendance is important for single parent families because church attendance

- is the most significant predictor of marital stability,
- is closely related to sexual restraint in teens,
- is associated with lower crime rates, and
- contributes to lower use of drugs and alcohol abuse.

What Can Your Church Do to Help the Children?

- Help them learn to study. Provide mentors. Show you care by asking them on Sunday, "How did that test go this week?"
- Encourage the single parent and child to attend worship services. Some single parents want to worship with their children, but in many churches everyone separates and goes their own way when they open the door. Make it possible for parents and kids to attend worship together.
- Show children in single-parent homes what Christian marriages look like. Think of putting a strong Christian married couple together with a single-parent family. In the book *Bakers Handbook of Single Parent Ministry*, Doug Dees talks about a family grafting program.[19] He finds a two-parent family that has children about the age of the single-parent family. He explains that the two-parent family helps the single parent see

how a normal two-parent family operates and acts. On holidays, invite single parents to the adopted home. By grafting the single-parent family into the strong two-parent family, they can all work together in close coordination in almost all areas. This is especially helpful for the single mom with a son or a single dad with a daughter.

• Offer the single mom or dad help and suggestions on discipline.

What Type of Family Did Jesus Encourage?

Jesus never endorsed a particular family form. Instead, he gave us examples of how the church constitutes our primary family. In three gospels, Jesus declares that his brothers and mother do the will of the heavenly Father. "Then he looked at those seated in a circle around him and said, 'Here are my mother and my brothers!'" (Mark 3:34).

Dr. Rob Rienow's parents divorced when he was in high school. He understands all the challenges single parents face. In an article, "Bible-Driven Ministry to Single Parents," he says that churches need to encourage church families to open their homes.[20] He quotes Acts 2:46: "Day by day continuing with one mind in the temple, and breaking bread from house to house, they were taking their meals together with gladness and sincerity of heart" (NASB). Rob says single parents need to have their relational needs met, and this can be done by building genuine Christian relationships and being welcomed into the lives and homes of other families in the church.

In order to help the single-parent family, you have to get them into your church before you can minister to them.

Tips for the Family-Friendly Church

• Have reserved parking spaces. Think of a single dad with a toddler, diaper bag, toys, and so on who is also trying to hold onto a five-year-old while walking a long distance to get to the church building. Single parents are notorious for running late.

- Have parking attendants and greeters at the door. One church has parking attendants who park the cars; another person takes the single parents around and walks them to their class and then picks them up after class to help them find their children and their car.

- Start a mentoring program for boys without a dad in the home. Or pair up the daughter of a single dad with an older woman in the church or a single female adult in the church.

- Bring in guest speakers who can speak to the hearts of single parents about parenting alone, budgeting, and even dating.

- Form Bible study groups on Sundays for single parents.

- Ask single parents to serve in ministry. You may think that your church already does this, but there are many single parents who simple need to be asked because they won't volunteer.

Ten Things Single Parents Want Leaders to Know

1. Help us feel included in the overall church family. A friendly smile and an invitation to sit with you will go a long way in encouraging us to feel included and welcomed.

2. Include us in viable ministry work in the church. We still have talents we can use for the Lord even if we are divorced or widowed or never married.

3. When you invite us to sing in the choir, come early to be a greeter, work in the food pantry, or other projects, remember to provide a nursery and child

care as we have no one to leave our children with at home.

4. Don't ask us to work in the nursery. We are on 24/7 with our own kids, and we are doing it without help.

5. Don't ask us to serve or host married couples' events. We might not have a valentine or plans for Valentine's Day, but asking us to host the married couples really hurts our morale.

6. Help us prepare for holidays like Christmas. One church set up a Christmas Creation time. This was set up on a Saturday before Christmas, and single parents could drop off their kids for the entire day. The kids were allowed to make Christmas presents for each parent, bake cookies for Christmas, and make Christmas tree decorations.

7. Help us be better parents by hosting parenting classes or bringing in a speaker who will speak on how to parent alone.

8. Assist us when we have a crisis. Many times we have no family close by to help and comfort us. But please don't send a married man to assist a single mom. We don't feel comfortable unless his wife accompanies him.

9. Remember us on Mother's Day and Father's Day, two of the most difficult celebrations for us as single parents. For some of us they are a yearly reminder that the union that created our children did not survive. For some it is a reminder that we failed.

10. Invite me to come along with your family when our kids take part in the same after-school activities. Any idea how lonely it is to sit at a track meet, a band concert, or a football game by yourself?

Ten Things Children of Divorce Need from Church Leaders

1. Caring adults who "understand that children from single parent homes may have a constant fear about their safety."

2. Adults who "will not leave them at the foot of the cross but will continually teach them about a heavenly Father who will never leave them or forsake them."

3. Adults who "understand the child standing before them may attend two different churches, two entirely different denominations and may be very confused about two different sets of belief."

4. Adult leaders who "understand the mourning process a child of divorce experiences."

5. Adults who "understand the grieving process single parents experience when they become a single parent."

6. Adults who "understand the child from a single parent home may live in two separate homes."

7. Church leaders who "understand the need to develop caring relationships with not only the child but also with the single parent."

8. Adults who "understand the single parent does not always have control over when the child will be able to attend various church events."

9. Adults in children's ministries who will "minister to the single parent as well as to the child."

10. Children's leaders who "understand the stages a single parent experiences as they parent their children alone."[21]

Ten Ways to Pray for Children of Divorce and Their Families

1. Pray for the child's state of confusion. Children of divorce live in a confused state for a long time after their parents separate. This happens mainly because no one is talking to the child about what is happening.

2. Pray for their feelings of safety. Almost every child of divorce doesn't feel safe at least part of the time after one of their parents move out of the home.

3. Pray for the child to realize the divorce is not their fault and is between two adults.

4. Pray for the child's comfort as he/she travels back and forth between homes. Realize that every time a child says "hello" to one parent, they have to say "good bye" to the other parent.

5. Pray for communication between the child and each parent. Because the parents are on stress overload, many times they unknowingly don't listen to their child or they retreat to their bedrooms to be alone and think.

6. Pray for the child's schoolwork as it usually suffers because the child can't concentrate or focus on studies or homework when their family is falling apart.

7. Pray for peace. Many children feel they are living in a war zone. They need the peace of Christ to fill their lives.

8. Pray for connections at church to be maintained and new connections created.

9. Pray for each parent to hear the call of God on their lives.

10. Pray for the child to come to a realization that there is a Father who will never leave them or forsake them.[22]

Nontraditional Families Are the New Normal

*Therefore lift your drooping hands and strengthen your weak knees,
and make straight paths for your feet, so that what is lame
may not be put out of joint but rather be healed.*

—Hebrews 12:12-13 RSV

Blended Families and Stepfamilies

Blended families and stepfamilies are on the increase. A step/ blended family is a marriage in which one or both parents become a stepparent to children that are not their own. Mental health specialists estimate that it takes anywhere from four to eight years for these families to become cohesive units. However, many blended families will end up divorcing before that time.

Statistics

Some research estimates that 65 to 70 percent of remarriages with children will fail. Forty percent of married couples with children in the United States are stepfamilies,[1] and "approximately one-third of all weddings in America today form stepfamilies."[2]

It is estimated that soon there will be more stepfamilies than traditional families. Most single parents will remarry before they have taken time to grieve the breakup of their previous marriage and heal from the previous marriage. Even if the parents have healed and moved on, many of their children have not. For years some children will harbor the idea that their birth parents will get back together. Many will try to sabotage the new marriage. Others will go into the new marriage thinking the new dad or mom is going to be the fairy godparent and give them everything they want. All of these elements can create havoc on the new marriage.

Some research shows that fewer than 30 percent of blended families are in the church. For those families that do attend church, most don't attend on a regular basis. In an interview, Paige and Moe Becnel said,

> One thing we hear from Blended Families over and over is that they think they are second class families in the church. They don't believe that the church takes them seriously. When they begin to have problems, they often see churches pass them on to a professional counselor, often a non-Christian, rather than trying to help and support them from within the church. So, they often wind up thinking that they are alone on this journey, even within the church walls.[3]

Ron Deal,[4] a leading expert on step and blended families, says for the most part churches rarely have a ministry for this population: "Traditional marriage and family educational resources prove inadequate to help prevent divorce and strengthen stepfamily homes. But ministry specifically designed for stepfamilies is helping couples beat the odds and break the cycle of divorce while helping churches become relevant to this growing population of families in their community."[5]

What Churches Can Do to Support Blended Families

From an interview with Moe and Paige Becnel we learn to do the following:

- Educate on-staff pastors who counsel couples, children, and youth about the unique issues blended families face and the proper guidance to help those families. Helping blended families heal helps the children in those families heal—positively affecting the next generation.
- A premarriage education for a blended family needs to have three or four blended family sessions that expose the potential key issues that undermine blended families and provide biblical solutions (not coping skills).
- Have education for remarried families in the form of semi-annual classes to help them overcome the issues that are unique to blended families.
- Include blended family breakout segments whenever a marriage conference is held.
- Conduct annual or semiannual blended family seminars to reach out to the unchurched blended families in the community, letting them know they are valued in the kingdom of God.
- Host ongoing life-groups (such as home groups, cell groups) for blended families, where they can meet, fellowship, and learn from other blended families.[6]

Educating church staff and volunteers includes teaching and letting them know there are many reasons stepfamilies struggle to pull together. Sometimes both partners bring children from a previous marriage into the family. Many parents assume the children are going to be as excited as they are to form this new family, but most adults fall in love and marry too soon after a divorce or the death of a spouse and before the children have had long enough to heal. Parents tend to forget they can fall in love with someone else but the other parent will always be the child's other parent.

Navigating the Minefield

I once worked with a stepfamily in which each parent brought children into the new marriage. The children from the mom consistently visited their dad on the first and third weekends. The children from the father visited their mom sporadically. The children were in a constant state of confusion as to who was going be where on what day. The mom's children were upset on the weekends they left mom at home with the dad's children. The dad's children were jealous that the mom's children got to see their other parent on a regular basis.

This family needed a healthy Christian family in the church to mentor them and help them navigate this minefield. Instead, they were treated like a traditional two-parent family. The children were all called by the stepdad's last name. Children and youth workers threw out questions about where their brother or sister was on the weekends the children visited their other parent. The kids were embarrassed when they had to continually repeat, "At the other house." Not one family member of this stepfamily felt the church leaders and congregation understood their family's situation.

Dr. Jeff Paraziale says, "Stepfamilies live in a constant state of 'relational overload.' Step-relationships are far more numerous and complex than first-time families."[7] In many families children live part time with their mother and part time with their father. Their schedule can be so confusing that an adult child once told me that he just kept his suitcase packed all the time. He said not until he went off to college did he feel like he could unpack. He said the stepparents would say, "Go upstairs and unpack your bag." He would go upstairs and lay his suitcase on the bed but never unpack. Both of his parents remarried. Both brought children into the home. Both brought confusion into their lives.[8]

Five Things Stepfamilies Need from a Church

1. Church leaders with a tender heart toward stepfamilies and their unique struggles and who will not label these families.

2. Children and youth leaders who have a workable knowledge of the problems children from stepfamilies face on a daily basis.

3. Children and youth workers who take the time to learn each child's last name. There may be three children in a family, each with a different last name—hers, his, and theirs!

4. Ministers who, when preaching out of the Old Testament, recognize the many stepfamilies in the Bible and will take time to reference these varied family types in their sermons.

5. Premarital counseling designed specifically for remarriages with children.

Grandparents Parenting Again

More and more grandparents are filling in as primary caregivers for their grandchildren. Many of these grandparents are single or they are in a second marriage and the entrance of grandchildren into the home strains the second/blended family. Some have waited years to enjoy their retirement and are concerned that they will never be afforded this opportunity. Others are busy and heavily involved in their careers. Many don't have the space in their homes to accommodate young children. Many do not have the financial resources to provide what the children need.

In many of these households, the grandparents care for children whose parents cannot or will not care for them because of any of the following:

- Substance abuse
- Illness
- Death of a spouse
- Abuse
- Neglect

- Economic hardship
- Imprisonment
- Divorce
- Domestic violence
- Natural disasters
- War/military duty
- Other family crisis

Several years ago I was climbing out of my car at the Ridgecrest Conference Center in North Carolina. Before I had even gotten my suitcase out, a friend in ministry to singles came running up to me and said:

> Oh Linda, I'm so glad you are here. I have a real dilemma and no-where to turn to find help. My husband's daughter has gotten herself in a big jam and it looks like we might be getting custody of her two children. I am not prepared for this. As a matter of fact, I'm pretty mad and upset about this. You know I raised my kids as a single mom. And I raised them in the church and in the Lord. I sacrificed by giving up speaking engagements and other things to be at home with my children and raise them to be responsible adults. I'm a grandmother now and I don't want to raise someone else's kids at this age in my life.
>
> It's not my fault my husband's ex-wife raised her kids the way she did. These are my husband's grandchildren and he thinks we should take these two children because if we don't they will have to go into state foster care. This is causing some real problems in our marriage. Can you help me? I don't know where to turn.

My friend was facing many issues. If these grandchildren came to live in her home, her life was going to change in ways she hadn't even recognized yet.

The Numbers

The 2000 Census was the first time questions about grandparents providing care were included. Results showed that from 1990 to 2000 there had been a 30 percent increase in grandparents as primary care-givers. It was estimated at the time of the 2000 Census that half of the grandchildren being parented by grandparents were under the age of six. In 2010, 2.7 million grandparents were responsible for the basic needs of one or more grandchildren under 18 living with them:

- 1.7 million were grandmothers, and 1.0 million were grandfathers;
- 5.4 million children under 18 were living in a grandparent household.[9]

These are only the reported numbers. Many families keep this information quiet. Perhaps some grandparents don't want to admit to the fact that they are rearing the next generation, or maybe they are hoping it will only be temporary.

When I was giving a presentation for the Association of Marriage and Family Ministries on grandparent care and what churches needed to know, halfway through the workshop a minister stopped me. He looked across the room at another minister from his church and said, "I had no idea that this is what some of our grandparents are facing. This accounts for why Mr. and Mrs. So-and-So quit coming to church on a regular basis. My goodness, they are exhausted!" He went on to explain that he noticed this couple had resigned some of their church positions right after the grandchildren came to live with them. Then he noticed they only attended sporadically. He said that he regretted his church had very little knowledge about this subject. And now he felt the church had abandoned this family.

Something ministers and church leaders need to know is the grandchildren—the children of the second generation—usually have different and more issues than their parents.

From my own observation over the years of working with grand-parents parenting again, I have come to the following conclusions:

- The child may be socially and emotionally delayed.
- The child may have no social skills and or lacks family interaction skills.

- The child may be grieving the death of a parent.
- If abuse has occurred, then the child may have trust issues.
- Children may have been exposed to antisocial behaviors.
- Children may not feel safe.
- No matter how children are treated by the grandparents, they still love and miss their parents.

Grandparents can't parent the second generation like they did the first. Grandchildren have more exposure to the world now than ever before. How are grandparents going to handle the Internet and violent music, TV, games, and movies? Many experts have concluded that because children are involved in these various medias they

- may become less sensitive to the pain of those around them,
- may become more fearful of their world, and
- may act more aggressively or harmfully to those around them.

10 Things Grandparents Parenting Again Need from the Church

1. Someone to provide respite care for the grandparents, especially for single grandparents.

2. Someone to help them check into the state's service agencies that help families get assistance. Check into SSI for special needs financial assistance. Check into Title XX for childcare assistance.

3. Churches that can provide resources where access to legal aid or legal representatives can be found. If the grandparent has not been given legal guardianship, the parents can retrieve their children without permission from the grandparent. Many states allow for kinship care, which gives the grandparents the legal rights to care for the grandchildren.

4. Churches to provide parenting classes on parenting children with challenging behavioral and emotional issues.

5. A church family who will intercede in prayer for the entire family—grandparent, parents, and child.

6. Churches to provide lay leadership to mentor and love these children and encourage the grandparents.

7. Churches that teach everyone in ministries about the legacy these children are going to have and how a church family can help avert or change the outcomes for the children.

8. Someone outside the family to pray with the children. Pray for their *comfort* and the comfort and safety of the missing parent. We forget to pray for the child's comfort. Stress causes much pain and discomfort for these children.

9. Churches that will provide, or find a neighboring church that will provide, a children's group support program such as DC4K, DivorceCare for Kids.[10]

10. Churches that can provide clothes and school supplies and even assist with providing children's furniture for bedrooms the children will be using.

The Boomerang Generation

As Brandi stepped out of her car, she nervously looked toward the church. This was Brandi's first time to attend this church. She had been out of church for a while and was searching for a place where she could get herself right with the Lord. Goodness knows, she had a lot on her plate with her daughter getting ready to go off on her own. And now her son was returning home with his girlfriend and their baby. As Brandi got lost in her thoughts, a nice older lady came alongside her and welcomed her to this church. Brandi found a welcoming church that had programs for her. She no longer felt strange with her family situation. She felt she belonged, and she soon began taking a more active role in the church.

Boomerang families are the families in which adult children are returning to the parental home to nest. It might be because they have graduated from college and haven't found a job. It might be because of a divorce. It might be because of underemployment, which means the adult child can't afford his or her own place.

In addition to the adult child's adjustments, the parents also have many adjustments to make. Many parents feel strange or judged in the church. Having children return home doesn't have to be seen as a failure on the part of the parents or the adult children. It is what it is and shouldn't be judged by fellow church members. Brandi was blessed that she found a church that didn't judge her but welcomed her with open arms.

From a CNN report we learn: "Overall, 39% of adults ages 18 to 34 say they either live with their parents or moved back in at some point in recent years." [11] This is a large population and an opportunity for the church to reach out. Keep in mind that some of these boomerang kids are moving back home with a family or as single parents with their children.

These adult children are not going to fit right back into the church they attended growing up. They have been away for years; they have changed a lot and may have outgrown the classes they previously attended. Their needs have changed, and the outlook some have on serving has changed. Have them complete a spiritual assessment inventory or find out what their spiritual gifts are by talking to them. Plug them into ministry. Your church can fill a need in their lives by giving them a place to serve. Some boomerang adults may need support ministries such as divorce or grief support small groups. Others may need financial support in the form of helpful budgeting classes or in finding employment. Their parents may need assistance understanding the needs of their adult children.

Steve Johnson, who is the founder and lead consultant for Etchea Coaching, and who has fifteen years of experience serving families in a church setting, says:

Provide care and a positive disposition for single adults who return to live with their parents. This is becoming more common and does not have to be seen as a shortcoming of the adult child. There are many good reasons for an adult to live with parents, but there are also different kinds of relational concerns that must be addressed for both the adult child and the parent.[12]

If they are single and have been away from home for several years, they may not fit into that twenty-something singles group. Many are coming home with college degrees. Many have worked in the corporate world. They want more than the meet-and-greet type of events they went to years ago. Some are searching for where they belong. They may be questioning the economy that is forcing them to return home. Some want deep religious studies and events where they can continue learning. Many want to share their knowledge. They want to connect. They want to be encouraged. They want to belong and not be made to feel inadequate because they have come home.

Single Adults in the Church

Today it is estimated that there are more single adults in our country than married adults. Even though adult singles are a growing demographic in our communities, most churches do not minister to them. There are a few larger churches that might have a viable ministry, but for the most part single adults are left out of church family.

Who are the single adults?

- Younger never-married adults. Many of these single adults are postponing marriage.
- Single parents who have never married.
- Older widows or widowers.
- Divorced adults who may or may not have children living in their home.

Many churches will say they don't have single adults in their church. However, if you take a good look, the numbers you find in your own congregation may surprise you. Kris Swiatocho, one of the few people developing ministry tools and working with churches to develop ministries to single adults, says,

- Look at your existing membership/attendance rolls and see who is not married. Categorize by age, past marital status, if they have kids that live at home or grown, and so on.
- Contact your town/city and find out the demographics of those living within a five-mile radius. Once you find out this information, it will help you understand how to reach them. You may find out you have a lot of single moms or widows. Depending on what you have the most of could determine whom you try to reach and how you minister to them.[13]

Don't know where to start looking for resources? A good place to start is at Kris's website, http://www.thesinglesnetwork.org.

Singles, no matter why they are single, should be included in the church family. Many times they are left out simply because they do not fit the church's idea of family. Yet when you look at the Bible, what do you see in Jesus? Wasn't he single? Jesus Christ is an example to every single wanting to stay active in worship.

Single people bring a lot of talent and resources to a church. Many of them bring a lot of revenue. I've known some very wealthy single adults. They want to belong and, if a church embraces them, they will give way beyond their tithe:

- They will give to causes. Many will anonymously support kids and youth activities.
- They will pay for church camps for kids who can't afford it.
- They will purchase musical instruments or purchase supplies for the youth and children's ministries.

If you reach out to singles, you might be surprised how much your church could benefit. Embrace them as part of the church family. This doesn't necessarily mean you need to start a large single-adult group. It does mean you need to be intentional about helping adult singles feel welcomed.

Kris Swiatocho says ministers tell her they don't want to start a singles group because they might be accused of starting a dating service. She says most singles go to church to worship, not to look for a date. She goes onto say, "But so what if they meet someone? What better place to meet a date or a future mate than in the Lord's house?"

The family minister, coach, and blogger for the Etchea site, Steve Johnson, makes a lot of sense when he says:

- View singles as whole numbers. They aren't partial people waiting for a spouse to complete them. Christ is their completion.
- Lift up single leaders in the church so that those joining your church do not feel marriage is a requirement for full membership.
- Develop a culture where families and singles mix regularly.
- Make an extra effort to see that singles are enveloped in the fellowship and discipleship groups of the church.[14]

Whether your community is made up of blended families or stepfamilies, grandparents parenting again, boomerang families, or singles, there should be no lack of potential members for your church. And we haven't even covered other nontraditional and conflicted family units.

Chapter 6

Other Common Family Structures

See what great love the Father has lavished on us,
that we should be called children of God!

—1 John 3:1

Adult Children of Divorce

Since the mid-seventies when divorce became rampant, millions of children have grown up in divorced homes. It is estimated that 25 percent of adults in their twenties and thirties spent at least part of the first eighteen years of life in a divorced home. As a minister preparing to marry a couple, it is prudent to inquire if either person was raised in a divorced home. If so, you will need to think through the process of how you might conduct your premarital counseling.

Educate yourself on how the divorce from childhood impacts the adults of today. For example, what do adult children and their spouses say are the pitfalls of growing up in a divorced home?

Do you realize some adult children of divorce have a well-rehearsed ability to hide their emotions? They have done this for years. Someone needs to help them change or even recognize it so they can be successful at living in an emotionally healthy marriage. Many have trouble understanding the concept of loving unconditionally.

Some adult children of divorce carry over hostilities and other divorce legacies into the marriage. Divorce issues may very well skew the adult child of divorce's perspective and outlook on relationships and marriage. Several experts, such as Judith Wallerstein, have researched and studied the divorce legacy for today's children and tomorrow's future.[1]

They have learned that children of divorce are at a higher risk as adults for

- anxiety and depression,
- personality and conduct disorders,
- promiscuity,
- substance abuse,
- becoming divorced as adult themselves,
- cohabitation and putting off marriage,
- health problems, and
- not attending religious services as adults.

Elizabeth Marquardt has done a national study on adult children of divorce.[2] One of the major issues in her findings was a strong connection between children of divorce and belief in God. Many said it was a lonely journey with not much support at home. These children had questions about God and spiritual issues but nowhere to turn for answers, as most single parents dropped out of church after the divorce.

Several years ago I was visiting with a mother who had a grown adult son. This mother had divorced her husband when her son was very young. She said to me:

> You know I had to move around a lot when Frank [name has been changed] was a child. He was the oldest of my three boys. And it didn't make any difference where we moved to, the first thing Frank did was look for a church. And it didn't make any difference what denomination it was. If it were close enough for him to walk to it, he would go to that church. And he would drag his two little brothers along with him.

How sad to think of this little eight- or nine-year-old boy on his own looking for a church. When talking to this man, he recalls that he didn't know anything about religion but he knew he wanted to go to church. In his adult years he no longer attended church. He believed he was saved, and periodically he would pray, but he no longer looked for a church.

As we develop a deeper understanding of the long-term affect divorce has on the adults in our congregations and in our communities, we are finding many of them are pulling away from the Lord in their adult years. In my observation, many are immature Christians frozen in a spiritual state of where they were as children when the divorce happened. Spiritually, many children stop developing after the divorce, never to develop a faith walk or a level of trust that the Lord desires from each of us. They tend to carry over anger toward the earthly parent to their relationship with God, the heavenly Father.

Many of these adults can't understand what a marriage relationship should look like because their parents never modeled it for them. If they can't understand a marriage relationship, how can they comprehend the relationship of Christ to his bride, the church?

> Husbands, go all out in your love for your wives, exactly as Christ did for the church—a love marked by giving, not getting. Christ's love makes the church whole. His words evoke her beauty. Everything he does and says is designed to bring the best out of her, dressing her in dazzling white silk, radiant with holiness. And that is how husbands ought to love their wives. They're really doing themselves a favor—since they're already "one" in marriage. (Ephesians 5:25-28 *THE MESSAGE*)

Become Cognizant about the Needs of the Spouse of the Adult Child of Divorce

Spouses need:

- To know the overall background of how family life was before the divorce.

- To understand what family life was like in both homes (if the children had access to both homes) after the divorce.
- To know the relationship between the mother and child.
- To understand the relationship between the father and child.
- To have some understanding of how the relationship with the parents is going to affect their marriage. For instance if the daughter grew to not trust her father, how is her relationship with her dad going to affect the relationship with her husband?
- To know how to find out about the adult child of divorce's fears when he or she won't talk about the fears or recognize them.
- Understand how to combat the one big fear the adult child of divorce has—that he or she will end up divorced and will put his or her own children through the same difficulties he or she went through as a child.
- Understand how to help their children have a relationship with both grandparents if there is no relationship between the adult child of divorce and a parent.[3]

Ten Things Adult Children of Divorce Want from a Minister

1. "If a minister is going to help me, I want them to have experienced divorce in some way, either as a child, an adult, or walked through it with a close friend. I don't think they can help me if they don't understand where I'm coming from. Or find someone that has been there and encourage him or her to walk with me. It's the perception thing."[4]

2. "Help me understand the scriptures and the Bible stories when I can't relate to a Heavenly God as a parent because my parent left me."

3. "Change your approach to some stories, studies, prayers, and activities to include and accommodate the child of divorce. As a teen, I always felt left out when the sermons on families only talked about two-parent families. I lived in a Christian single-parent family but was made to feel I didn't have a family."

4. "How can adults that have had a parent desert them understand John 3:16, "For God so loved the world that he gave his only begotten Son, that whoever believed in him should not perish but have everlasting life"? Explain that to me in terms I can understand."

5. "Because our parents demonstrated that there were limits to forgiveness, how can we believe that God does not maintain those same limitations?"[5]

6. "Help us understand that God can love us and he will never forsake us as our earthly parent did. Teach us that God's word has power and we can use his word to heal from our childhood."

7. "Help us understand the Holy Spirit. We need to know that the Holy Spirit can pour out God's love in us. We need to realize the Holy Spirit can and does intercede with God for us with sighs and moans too deep for words."

8. "Teach us to pray."

9. "Hold your congregations together when one person leaves because they want a divorce. Children are seeing the death of their once-intact family; they don't need to witness the church taking sides and falling apart. They need to see prayerful concern and God's love extended toward the family."

10. "Help your congregants to survive and understand how to pray for and minister to all parties, including the children."[6]

Some adult children of divorce can also be emotionally imma-ture because divorce can disrupt normal development, including emotional, physical, social, and spiritual development. They may need spiritually mature, emotionally healthy, and happily married couples to mentor them.

DivorceCare4Kids (DC4K) is a program created to help elemen-tary-age children heal from the devastation divorce brings into their lives.[7] Many of the DC4K leaders are adult children of divorce. They tell me they continue to heal as they help younger children. Plus, the children are encouraged as they come to know that the adults have experienced the divorce of their parents and they are doing okay. It is a rare and special connection between the child of divorce and the adult child of divorce. Robyn Besemann sums it up pretty well when she says, "The pain and damage of a parent's divorce includes issues of trust, abandonment, betrayal, loyalty, loneliness and more. The older a person gets, the easier it is to put the pain aside and just 'live life.' What happens many times, however, is that those issues arise again and again throughout life and negatively affect many areas of a person's life."[8] Help them heal and contribute to your church fam-ily. Encourage them to tell their stories to others. Allow them to use their hurts to help others who are experiencing divorce.

Boomers and Beyond Group

You may be hearing a lot about the baby boomers right now. That's because by the end of 2014, the last of the 77.5 million boom-ers will turn fifty.[9] Boomers are the people who were born between 1945 and 1964. I'm one of the older boomers, born in 1947. All my life my generation has done things differently. At the time we were born we were the largest generation to come along. We were the six-ties, the hippies, and the demonstrators. We brought in bell-bottom pants, short skirts, the women's liberation movement, long hair on men, women in the workforce, and free love. Well, I didn't bring in free love, but a lot of my friends did.

We were involved in the Vietnam conflict, with many dying in combat. We were marchers in the Civil Rights movement. We were the Watergate generation and the Woodstock generation. We set out to change the world. And change the world we did.

Starting in elementary school we were crammed into schools that weren't prepared for the onslaught of first graders that showed up. Every year from 1952 on, baby boomers caused havoc in the local schools. With the numbers swelling, principals and administrators scrambled to find enough teachers and space to provide for us.

Churches were not prepared for us either. By the time I came along, the nurseries in churches had started growing. With each grade I entered, our church swelled in the numbers of children in attendance. It seemed like we were always in large groups. From first grade through high school, we paved the way. When we became teenagers, churches formed youth groups. The ministers tried to keep us entertained and tried to get us all "saved." We went to church camps in large groups. We got baptized in large groups.

Now we are starting to retire, and we are still changing our world, with Social Security and Medicare scrambling to accommodate us. We join the ranks of the older generation and the senior adults. But don't call us "senior" adults, because we scoff at it.

It is estimated that for the next eleven years eleven million people will turn sixty-five years of age. When I was on the phone talking to the Medicare staff recently, they told me that they have more than eight thousand people a day applying for Medicare. But the saddest part of our demographic is that we are not attending church. On his website, Thom Rainer says, "But here is the harshest reality about my generation. We estimate that only about one-third of Baby Boomers are Christians. That means that 50 million adult Americans in this generation are unchurched and have yet to be reached with the gospel of Christ."[10]

Remember I said ministers tried to get us "saved"? Many boomers walked the isle to the altar simply because their friends did. Now in their retirement years, many don't know God and have a disdain for religion. While many don't attend church, the good news is that many will come *if* they are invited.

Other people think boomers might start looking more toward the local church as they age. What might explain why a boomer would become more religious? Part of it may be simply a function of maturation. "Marriage, having children, homeownership, and simply having roots in a community are all factors that nudge people toward religion," David E. Campbell, a Notre Dame professor who wrote *American Grace* with Robert D. Putnam, said in an e-mail.[11]

Then there is that other little matter: mortality, says Wade Clark Roof, professor of religion and society at the University of California, Santa Barbara.[12] What may explain why a boomer would become more religious? Part of it may be simply a function of maturation. "Marriage, having children, homeownership, and simply having roots in a community are all factors that nudge people toward religion," David E. Campbell, the Notre Dame professor who wrote *American Grace* with Robert D. Putnam, said in an e-mail.[13] The article explains that as parents and friends begin to die off, boomers are beginning to realize they are not immortal. Many are facing mortality with a new appreciation, and this can give churches an open window of opportunity to reach them.

There are not many churches developing ministries for this population. Several years ago when my family had to face the realities of placing our mom in an assisted living facility, I had one minister who helped me. He is one of the few I've come across who knows how to minister to boomers and the older generation.

Example of Boomer Ministry

James Craver is with First Baptist Church in Allen, Texas.[14] James leads seminars all over the country, and he helps churches start ministries for boomers and beyond. He speaks about how, first of all, we are trying to get boomers into the church the wrong way. We can't do this kind of ministry like we used to do it even ten years ago. And he clarifies that seniors include more than just boomers.

James says,

> As sociologists monitor the country's shifting demographic patterns, a most fruitful opportunity for outreach is emerging. Nearly eight thousand people a day in the United States are turning sixty years old, and the "mature adult" population is exploding at three times the national population growth rate.

Approximately 58 percent of these older Americans have no religious affiliation. And, according to religious conversion research, they are entering one of the most receptive times of their life for spiritual change. Unfortunately, the great majority of today's churches are unprepared for this "age wave."

It is important to get to know this group of people and what will bring them to your church and keep them coming. They are independent. They like to learn new things. They like to own it. James Craver says he has observed that they like to come up with their own ideas and then take ownership.

Other Boomer Traits

- They are cause driven.

  - They prefer short-term projects such as
  - mission trips to local schools to furnish school supplies;
  - backpack buddies—backpacks packed with food for kids to take home from school;
  - mentoring; and
  - summer school lunch ministries.

- They want immediate results.
- They are tolerant.
- They want multiple choices in life.
- They are experience oriented.
- They like informal settings.
- They believe women should be represented in leadership.
- They are open-minded.
- They believe church leaders should deal sensitively with hurting people.
- They are disillusioned with Christians who have been hypocritical throughout their lives by having affairs, robbing the corporate world, and so on.

Here are some warnings and don'ts that James Craver has learned over the years of working with older adults:

- Don't call them seniors. If you promote any activity with the word *seniors* in it, they won't come.
- Drop the "clubs" like Triple L Club. Clubs are exclusive and many think they will have to pay to belong to a club.
- Stop the monthly luncheons. They do not like potluck dinners.
- On Sundays, if you do those opening assemblies, drop them.

James tells me about one man who refused to come back to church because they spent twenty minutes on announcements and then prayer time. When it came down to the teaching, the teacher only had fifteen minutes to teach God's word. James has dropped all opening assemblies at his church. Prayer sheets are given to everyone when he or she enters the room and each person is encouraged to record his or her prayer request on these pages. They don't make a lot of announcements but get right down to the teaching. This has increased their attendance on Sunday mornings.

In addition,

- Boomers won't take long trips, but they will go on day trips.
- They won't come to monthly meetings.
- They don't like boring speakers.

Boomers want to leave an event having learned something. These events should be boomer led:

- Computer courses
- Digital photography
- Workshops and seminars on

- schemes and scams,
- living larger in smaller spaces, and
- caregiving (cancer, Alzheimer's)

- Karaoke night

James shared with me that a couple of his men came to him with the idea of having a karaoke night at church. He said he remembers thinking to himself, "This is the dumbest idea I've ever heard of." But he went on to tell the men to go home and pray about it and come back in two weeks organized with everything they would need and an assistant. He wanted an assistant so that if the men had to be absent for any reason, there would be someone to step up.

The men came back with everything they would need, and they set a date to have their first session. They would meet once a month. The first night an eighty-two-year-old woman was one of the first to get up. She got up on the stage and started crying. Then she said, "All my life, since I was a little girl, I've wanted to sing into a microphone." As she sang, the entire group ended up weeping. Family was created, and everyone was accepted.

Boomers prefer to lead different events such as the following:

- Gospel Gathering
- Game nights
- Wii tournaments
- Exercise classes (usually 99 percent women)
- Nutrition classes

One event that James's church does is to allow boomers to go to local retirement centers (not nursing homes) on Sunday and lead the worship service. They present an entire worship service. He said the first time they went, the manager of the retirement center called him and asked what he was supposed to do with all the money. Seems as though the people were so appreciative they took up an offering.

Currently they are serving at five retirement centers, using one hundred volunteers, and they have more centers on the waiting list.

They are just waiting for more volunteers to step up. He said they bring in around three thousand dollars a month from the retired participants in the centers. While they don't do it for the money, it is great the retired people are able to support this ministry. Boomers take their grandchildren to help them. The younger children serve as greeters. The youth go to the centers on holidays and decorate.

After observing the popularity of serving in retirement centers, James stumbled onto another surprising development, and that was the results of allowing boomers to teach Sunday school and Bible study classes on a quarterly basis. This allows them to travel *and* serve in the church. Many go to see their grandkids for two or three weeks at a time, or they want to go on extended vacations. And there are snowbirds who like to go to warmer climates during the winter. This quarterly rotation also allows the classes in the church to have consistency. Boomers want lessons and sermons that are heavy on practical application so they can apply their faith to their daily lives.

First Baptist Church, Allen, Texas, encourages outreach and evangelism. Boomers are trained how to tell personal stories of their salvation and faith walk. They do this with former coworkers, friends, and neighbors. They do outreach and evangelism through

- men's/women's informal coffee clubs,
- book clubs,
- golfing outings with buddies,
- small-group interaction, and
- walking with neighbors on a daily basis.

Sixty percent of boomers are just waiting for someone to ask them to attend an event at church (not just at Christmas or Easter). We must remember that all of the boomer events that we have are open to the community.[15]

In many churches pastors only know about monthly luncheons, trips, and pastoral care. With boomers and older adults, you have to have a diversified ministry. Have more evening meetings than daytime ministries. Boomers are busy during the daytime volunteering in their community, babysitting grandchildren, or even working full- or part-time. Life activities, not Christmas and Easter programs, will bring them into the church. Reach them outside the walls of your church.

Other Boomer Traits

Unfortunately, boomers have the highest rate of divorce of any other age group.[16] It is a new phenomenon called the gray divorce. Hosting divorce recovery classes will bring these hurting people into your church. They don't need a special class just for their age group, but they will fit in mixed age groups. In the divorce recovery group at my church, we have a wide variety of ages. Bonds are created and community is formed.

Over 50 percent of boomers are single. Some are involved in risky behaviors such as binge drinking. Boomers also have a high rate of sexually transmitted diseases.[17] These negative traits are even more reason churches need to be diligent in reaching out to the boomer population.

There are many lonely boomers sitting in your community. Having left their marriages and their children earlier on, they created rifts in family ties. Their adult children don't have much contact with good old dad or mom. There are still feelings of hurt and betrayal, so these older men or women sit alone or move into retirement centers and nursing homes with no one to visit them on holidays and special days. What if they could renew their relationship with Christ or even come to truly know him for the first time in their lives? Your church might be the open door needed for the change in their lives.

From the article "Religion May Play More Prominent Role in America as Baby Boomers Age" by Matthew Brown, we read,

> Based on the premise that people become more religious as they age, Gallup editor-in-chief Frank Newport predicts that religion will have a more prominent place in American society as a new generation of seniors hits retirement age over the next 20 years. . . .
>
> Baby boomers have always had an impact on the religious, political, economic and social landscape of America, experts agree, and Newport argues that those institutions that capture the projected

religious zeal of the boomer generation as it grows older will have the advantage.[18]

Other Concerns about Families and Our World

Our world is full of conflicted families. It is important to stay abreast of national trends as well as state and local trends. One new development, which I pray doesn't become a trend, is happening in a few states that are trying to pass a law where three parents can appear on a child's birth certificate. How will your church handle a situation where a child with three legal parents shows up in one of your children's programs? Who will you contact if there is a problem with the child? How will you accommodate this child when it comes to making gifts for parents on special days? Will you have the supplies for a child to make three gifts?

Boomers, single parents, single adults, boomerang kids, grandparents parenting again, blended families and stepfamilies, families with children who have special needs—the list goes on and on. What an exciting time to be reaching out into our world today. Is our job any harder, though, than what the disciples faced after the death of Christ?

One who has unreliable friends soon comes to ruin,
  but there is a friend who sticks closer than a brother.
(Proverbs 18:24)

Isn't it time we introduced all the people in different family structures to the One who is closer than their earthly brothers?

Suggested Resources

Grandparents

"Grandparents Raising Grandchildren." USA.gov. http://www .usa.gov/Topics/Grandparents.shtml#Data_and_Publications.

Linda Ranson Jacobs. "Grandparents Parenting Again." hlp4 .com. 2009. http://www.hlp4.com/grandparents.html.

Adult Children of Divorce

Center for Marriage & Families. "Does the Shape of Families Shape Faith?." Institute for American Values. http://centerfor marriageandfamilies.org/shape-of-families/.

Boomers

Amy Hanson. "What Church Leaders Need to Know about Ministry to Aging Baby Boomers." *Leadership Network* (blog). July 12, 2010. http://leadnet.org/blog/post/what_church_leaders_need _to_know_about_ministry_to_aging_baby_boomers.

AmyHanson.org. http://amyhanson.org. Amy's ministry specializes on boomers. Amy reminds us that the most powerful and underutilized source of Kingdom impact is the fifty-and-over generation.

Angela Coleman. "How to Incorporate Baby Boomers in Your Church." Yahoo! Voices. Last modified February 8, 2013. http://voices.yahoo.com/how-incorporate-baby-boomers-church -11993094.html.

Deacon Greg Kandra. "Are Baby Boomers Headed Back to Church?" *Patheos* (blog). December 31, 2012. http://www.patheos.com/blogs/deaconsbench/2012/12/are -baby-boomers-headed-back-to-church//.

Eric Nagourney. "Why Am I Back in Church?" NYTimes.com. Last modified October 3, 2012. http://www.nytimes.com/2012 /10/04/booming/04question-booming.html?_r=0.

Chapter 7

Looks Count and So Do Church Attitudes

*Dear children, let us not love with words or tongue
but with actions and in truth.*

—1 John 3:18

What impression does your church give when visitors pull up in front? From the parking lot, grounds, lobby or foyer, and classrooms, to the sanctuary and back door, first impressions make an impact on people. Businesspeople say a lasting impression is formed within the first ten seconds upon entering a parking lot. Church consultants say guests decide if they are coming back within eight to eleven minutes of driving into the parking lot and walking into your building.

Keep in mind people pulling into your parking lot might be unchurched people. Many unchurched adults reach out during a crisis and many are turned off by the treatment they get at church. Looks count, and while looks include the facility and surrounding grounds, they also include the looks on faces inside. They include the attitudes and love that are mirrored from the heart.

Have you forgotten what it's like to be a first-time visitor to your church? When was the last time you took a critical look at your church? Take a trip through your church and see how it looks to an outsider. Or you could go the route of large retailers but instead of a "mystery shopper" you could ask someone outside your church to come and be the "mystery worshiper."[1]

A Lesson from Theme Parks

I go to a lot of conferences around the country. Many of these conferences are at theme parks like Disney World, and the first thing I notice are the signs that are posted everywhere. You don't have to wonder where the bathrooms are or where to purchase a drink. The parks are not only attractive but also clean and well groomed with attractive plants and decorations. You don't see any lopsided signs or out-of-date décor.

Something else I noticed is the way Disney, especially, treats the children. First of all, no matter who is checking in or walking through the gates of a Disney park, the children are noticed first. The adults are greeted warmly also.

Disney staff people are pleasant and accommodating to everyone. Most smile when talking to the children or to the adults. They are truly helpful people. Now you may be saying, "Well, of course they are helpful and smiling because it is their job to make the visitors welcomed. Their job depends on it." Isn't it our job to make visitors welcomed, too? Aren't lost souls our job? What if we changed our attitudes about how we welcome people to our church?

Here are some comparisons to consider:

- Are you accommodating to guests visiting your church by taking your time with them? Or do you send them wandering down the hallway, blindly looking for children's Sunday school classrooms or the nursery?
- Do you think guests should automatically understand the "churchese" language you are speaking? If they haven't attended church before, they may not understand your denominational terms and abbreviations. Perhaps it would be beneficial to your guests to provide them with a welcome packet explaining various terminologies. Or put the common terms and

abbreviations on your website where visitors will see them before they visit your church. When making announcements, use the full name instead of abbreviations. For example: "Tuesday night the M.M. group is meeting." Any idea what the M.M. group is? For this church, the M.M. group is the "Military Ministry." While this is a great ministry for people in the military, unless you were told in advance what M.M. stands for, you wouldn't show up on Tuesday night.

- Disney people bend down to shake the hands of the children. Do you take time to get on the children's level and offer them a greeting? Perhaps you give them some options of how they want to be greeted. Handshake? Fist bump? High five? A hug? If you want to win the parents over, take time with their children.
- Disney characters make a big deal of welcoming a child by asking him or her questions that are relevant to the child.
- Disney staff does not talk over the child's head, even when talking to the adults; they still keep eye contact with the child. Many times it is important to get information from the parent, but think about making eye contact or periodically looking over to the child. Perhaps even ask the child a question or two so that the child feels like he or she is contributing and not just being talked about.
- Disney people will even continue to smile at the child while talking to the adults.
- Disney people are savvy because they know who is going pull the strings attached to mom or dad's credit cards. Church children's volunteers could take a cue from Disney, because if a child likes coming to your church, she or he will pull the parents along with her or him.
- Disney staff always steps aside for customers. They wait for you to enter a door or walk down a sidewalk or hallway.

- They hold doors open for children and adults.
- They say "Excuse me" when they have bumped or walked in front of someone. They are polite to everyone, and they always smile.

You may be thinking that the Disney staff is trained, while all your greeters are just volunteers. Want guests to return to your church? Invest in your volunteers. Better yet, give them a name such as "The Greeters," "The Hospitality Team," or "The Hospitality Ministry Team," and train the people who serve in this area.

Change the mind-set in your church from the volunteers who stand at the door saying "Good morning," to the Hospitality Ministry that welcomes the guests to your church family. The Hospitality Ministry can become an important and critical part of helping first-time guests feel welcomed and at home. Remember, first-time guests decide if they will return to your church within the first eight to eleven minutes of their arrival. This is before they have heard the sermon or worshiped through the music, which by the way are the two elements where the most time is spent in preparation.

The leader of the Hospitality Ministry needs to develop a vision and be able to impart this vision to others about the importance of the ministry's purpose. He or she then needs to recruit and provide regular training for the ministry team. After all, the members of the Hospitality Ministry are the first people guests will interact with at your church.

Depending on the size of your church, the Hospitality Ministry can involve several volunteers. These can include the following:

- Greeters stationed at every entrance into the church building or buildings
- People stationed at a welcome center
- Ushers
- Parking lot attendants
- Valet greeters (person that opens the door for cars driving up to the front entrance)

- Roaming volunteers who are available to help guests or guide guests to other parts of the church such as the nursery or children's section

Geoff Surratt has a couple of innovative ideas.[2] The first is what he calls the "gorilla greeter" team. These are people who are friendly but don't wear name tags. Their challenge is to talk to people they don't know in the first ten minutes after the people arrive and for the first ten minutes after the service. Great idea! I've been in churches that should adopt this concept. I've entered churches where I was a guest speaker and have not had one person leave her or his peer group and talk to me. It is a very lonely world out there in some of our churches. Another idea is to "adopt a neighborhood." For this, he suggests that you divide your worship space into neighborhoods or sections. Find people who generally sit in those areas and challenge them to watch for "new neighbors" who might sit in their section.

A Look at Your Physical Facility

Just as church members need to critique how they welcome guests, it is important to take a critical look at the physical facility.

Parking Lot

- There need to be signs from the parking lot to the church and from the church to the parking lot. I have gotten lost in parking lots of churches while trying to navigate the maze of several parking lots. All I wanted was a sign telling me where to park for the church service.
- It is always a good idea to have spaces fairly close to the main entrance clearly marked for visitors or guests.

- Parking for individuals with disabilities needs to be clearly labeled and close to the main entrance.
- Parking spaces are brightly painted with fresh paint and are easy to see.
- Have clearly painted arrows pointing people to the exit when they are ready to exit the parking area.

Entrances

- Visitors need signs on the outside of the building to direct them to the worship space, fellowship hall, church offices, preschool, and so on. More than once, I've gone in a door I thought would lead me into the back of the worship area, only to go into the front by mistake.

Grounds and Landscaping

- Landscaping needs to look attractive and organized.
- Plants, flowers, and mulch or rocks need to look fresh.
- Dead plants speak volumes to some people. It conveys the thought, "If they don't care enough to water and care for their plants, how will they take care of my family?"
- While the lawn doesn't need to be a manicured lawn, it should look well maintained with the grass mowed and the sidewalks edged.
- Sidewalks should not be cracked or have large dips or holes in them.

Signs

- Do guest know where to turn in to your church from the main street? If you are not located on a major thoroughfare, there should be signs directing people from a major street to your church.

- Do guests know where to park? If you have more than one parking area, is the one for the guests easy to find? Is there a sign?
- Do guests know where the main door to the church is? Is the entrance clearly marked?
- Do guests know immediately where to go for more information?
- Do guests know where the children's area is located?
- Once guests have registered their young children and have them settled in, do they know how to find the way back to the adult area for classes or to the sanctuary?

The Church Interior

- Hallways need to be bright, cheerful, and attractive.
- Parents will want to know how to find their children in a maze of halls and classrooms, so attractive signs should be displayed.
- If your church is housed in several different buildings, provide a map so guests will be able to locate the different classrooms.
- If you have classrooms in other locations, provide covered walkways in between buildings. One church I visited had many different buildings. A couple of buildings were on the other side of the driveway. In the foyer of the main building there were large containers of umbrellas. On the day that I was at this church, it started raining. Everyone was encouraged to grab an umbrella. When you walked in the door of another building there were umbrella containers where everyone tossed their umbrellas. Members of the hospitality ministry held the umbrellas for older people, young single moms carrying children, or others who might have problems getting around. Talk about being

impressive. I thought, "If I ever move to this location, this is the first church I will visit." It felt warm and comforting, especially when I saw young men and youth holding umbrellas over people and opening the doors for young moms, older adults, and a person in a wheelchair.

Furniture and Children's Areas

- While it is not necessary to have the most up-to-date equipment and furniture, it is important that what you have looks attractive and is in good repair. There are companies that can install new décor or make suggestions to improve your current facility. If you want young families with children to become a part of your church, pay particular attention to your nursery. You will want to make sure that things like baby beds meet current safety standards.
- Currently, themed children's areas are all the rage, and there are companies that can help make suggestions. Themed areas can be as large and lifelike as you want. Hallways can be painted from floor to ceiling with murals of outdoor scenes, including large boulders, trees, green grass, and blue skies. Some companies sell mural kits. You can use 2D or 3D elements in your theme. You can use large stickers that attach to your walls. Posters and banners are another way to make your children's area look attractive. You can have an animal theme, a Noah's ark theme, or other biblical theme. You are only limited by your imagination and your budget.

Inspecting the Facilities

It is important to periodically have church facilities inspected. The following is a list to guide your inspection:

- Make sure all light fixtures are in proper working order.
- Replace lightbulbs that are burned out or flickering.
- Fix all bathroom doors and make sure they have latches on individual stalls.
- Check that bathroom toilet paper holders are in place and filled with toilet paper.
- Make sure paper towels and soap dispensers are full and in good working order.
- Provide trash receptacles throughout the church.
- Fix loose doorknobs.
- Make sure carpets are clean and not ripped or frayed.
- Walls should be clean with no chipping paint.
- Make sure that all stairs and steps (inside and outside) are clearly marked.

One church where I was a member periodically had a workday. In advance, the building and grounds group inspected the church building and grounds. They compiled lists of things that needed to be repaired, painted, or cleaned. Members were able to sign up in advance for the area they wanted to work. Volunteers brought tools, cleaning supplies, and donated painting supplies. This church also included the outside landscaping in their spring workday. Plants, flowers, and mulch were donated along with the labor to make the outside of the church look pleasant. Children and youth worked alongside all of the adults.

An amazing result of the workday was that everyone in the church (including the children and youth) took better care of this church as they took ownership of the church building. Another interesting thing happened: the youth became more involved with all the adults in the church, from their parents to the older adults. Young people also learned how to repair equipment, paint, and plant flowers and bushes. This was particularly special to the kids from single-parent homes.

You became imitators of us and of the Lord, for you welcomed the message in the midst of severe suffering with the joy given by the Holy Spirit. (1 Thessalonians 1:6)

Great first impressions don't just happen. Church leaders need to be attentive to specifics about the first impressions they want guests to have. People matter.

Ten Things Guests Need

1. Aesthetically pleasing entrance into the church.

2. Guest parking.

3. To be greeted with friendly faces, smiles, and a meaningful hello at the front door.

4. To connect with one or two people with whom they can relate.

5. Name tags on greeters, ushers, and other people they will come into contact with.

6. Attractive signage directing them to various parts of the church.

7. A well-kept and clean building.

8. Clean bathrooms with plenty of supplies.

9. Welcome packet with information pertinent to their visit.

10. Effective follow-up after their visit.

What Guests Don't Need

Do not ask visitors or guests to stand up and introduce themselves and tell where they are from. Most people are not public speakers and this act will only serve to make them feel uncomfortable.

Ten Ways to Get New Members to Connect

1. Share the church's vision with each new member.

2. Provide opportunities for the family to worship as a family unit. (In other words, don't separate families every time they walk in the door of your church.)

3. Provide new member packets that explain various ministry teams and programs, introduce all staff, explain particulars about your church or denomination, and provide explanations of various church terminologies and abbreviations.

4. Relationships are key, so provide ways for people to meet and connect with others through small groups, programs, Bible studies, ministries, and so on.

5. Give them opportunities to tell their stories and share their testimonies when they are ready and feel comfortable.

6. Provide one-page descriptions of all the ministries in your church.

7. If people want to serve, allow them to serve where they have gifts, talents, and passion. Don't pigeonhole them into the place where you have an opening and need a warm body. (Many people are waiting to be asked to serve, so don't wait for them to volunteer.)

8. For people who want to serve, make it easy for them to gradually join in ministry projects that are short term.

9. Provide training in the area of ministry in which they choose to serve.

10. Tell them thank you often for serving.

Suggested Resources

Hospitality

"Church Hospitality Resource Links." EvangelismCoach.org. Last modified May 10, 2010. http://www.evangelismcoach.org/church -hospitality/. This is an exhaustive list with many links to articles and videos.

Lavern Brown. "7 Simple Steps to First Rate Church Hospitality." *Pastors.com* (blog). January 21, 2013. http://pastors.com/7-simple -steps-to-first-rate-church-hospitality/.

Will Mancini. "Guests at Church: 10 Mind Blowing Facts to Fuel Your Hospitality Ministry." *Will Mancini* (blog). November 22, 2010. http://www.willmancini.com/2010/11/guests-at-church-10 -mind-blowing-facts-to-fuel-your-hospitality-ministry.html.

Children's Themes

NoogaBoogaScenic. "Children's Church Theming, Freedom Church, Gallatin, TN." YouTube. Last modified March 16, 2011. http://www.youtube.com/watch?v=oXrWbNrKQ1c. Video of Freedom Church in Gallatin, TN, children's themed area.

Randy Triplett. "Themed Children's Ministry Trends - 2011 And Beyond." Creative for Kids. http://www.creativeforkids.com /webapp/design-studio/church-decor-articles/183-themed-childrens -ministry-trends-2011-and-beyond.

"Welcome to Church Decor Articles." Creative for Kids. http:// www.creativeforkids.com/webapp/design-studio/church-decor -articles. Has several articles and ideas for children's themed areas.

Worlds of Wow (blog). http://worldsofwow.blogspot.com/. Several photos of children's themed areas.

Connecting New Members

"50 Ways to Build Strength in Participation." Lewis Center for Church Leadership. http://www.churchleadership.com/pdfs/50Ways/50_Ways_to_Build_Strength_in_Participation.pdf.

"50 Ways to Welcome New People." Lewis Center for Church Leadership. http://www.churchleadership.com/50Ways/NewPeople.html.

Heather Johnson. "How to Connect and Keep New People." *Outreach* Magazine. http://www.churchleaders.com/?news=138861/.

Chapter 8

Keeping the Family in Family Ministry

He decreed statutes for Jacob
and established the law in Israel,
which he commanded our ancestors
to teach their children,
so the next generation would know them,
even the children yet to be born,
and they in turn would tell their children.
Then they would put their trust in God
and would not forget his deeds
but would keep his commands.

—Psalm 78:5-7

Churches are realizing that changes need to be made to ministries and programs because of the many varied family types that they want to attract to their church. In order to bring cohesiveness to families, some churches are looking at merging various ministries under one title, family ministry. Leadership can pull all kinds of families together in an organized fashion so that families are encouraged to be a family at church and at home.

From the mid-1950s and into the first half of the 1960s, churches enjoyed a time of growth and prosperity. In the beginning of the 1950s, World War II was over and the world was enjoying relative peace for the first time in a long time. Churches enjoyed a time of prominence in the community. The majority of people in our country claimed to be Christian, even if they didn't attend a local church on a regular basis. When there was a family crisis, even nonchurched people turned to their local church for support.

Families attended church together. Families sat together in the church service. Children were included in all parts of the church events, including those long and boring business meetings. I remember those meetings. I recall that at the time I thought they were long and boring. Now I realize that I learned a lot about how adults interacted as Christian brothers and sisters, even when they disagreed. I observed how prayer really works. I learned about the inner workings of a church, and I came to understand the reason things were done a certain way. I learned the majority ruled and how, if you disagreed with the majority, you could either make a choice to accept or you could leave, but either way the majority ruled. I observed motions being made, discussions taking place, and how voting completed the process. In prayer meetings, as they were called, I learned how the church took care of its own. I observed what faith meant and how strong Christians lived out their faith daily. I saw Christian interactions:

- If someone needed food, food was delivered.
- If a family experienced a death, the church family surrounded the family.
- If someone went to the hospital, the church family showed up and people took turns providing support twenty-four hours a day.
- If someone lost his or her job, the church took up a collection to help out.
- If someone needed clothes, clothes magically showed up at his or her door.
- If someone got sick, hot meals were prepared and delivered to the family.

In using the word *family* I mean even young children learned to save their pennies and contribute. Children shared in the responsibility of donating clothes and preparing meals. Teens were active in contributing and serving in the church. Family included everyone, no matter her or his age.

While I'm not suggesting churches go back and replicate the church of that century, I think there are things we could learn from that generation. Somewhere along the way, we decided to throw out the baby with the bathwater, so to speak. Churches started separating families. Today when a family enters the doors of the church, everyone separates. Children go one way, teens go another way, each parent goes to his or her own class, and many family members don't see each other until they get in their car to leave. Actually, many families don't even arrive in the same car. How many cars does your family take to church?

I'm not saying any of this is particularly wrong or bad; what I am saying is at some point many churches lost a sense of being a church where

- family worship takes place together,
- communal prayers mean something,
- testimonies of answered prayers are heard by all ages,
- it is acceptable to share how God is working in one's life,
- scriptures are taught and come alive for people,
- rituals or points of emotional connection are formed,
- one can find a dependable community,
- everyone feels a responsibility to serve, and
- an intergenerational community of faith believers comes into the presence of God and lives by his word and under his authority.

New Concept

For many of us, family ministry is a relatively new concept. However, all one has to do is look back to the Bible to see this is not new. Children were included in worship and events throughout the Bible. Jesus encouraged the children to be brought to him.

In his book *Limited Church: Unlimited Kingdom*, Rob Rienow has included a section about children in worship in the Bible.[1] He starts with how God commanded parents to celebrate the Passover with their families. He walks us through various books of the Old Testament and then the New Testament where God spoke to the children. He gives many examples where children were included in the church and why reaching the family is important in our world today.

Many of us have been oriented in the program-based model. This is where ministries are launched without much thought about how they fit into the overall church plan, if there is a church plan. People come into a church with a talent or spiritual gift and are thrown into serving or creating a new ministry. The new ministry either fits under an existing minister or a new minister is hired to oversee it.

Granted, this provides people many choices of ministry options, but rarely does it bring cohesiveness to the church family. Everything just happens and ministers and leaders rarely come together. Many times the right hand doesn't know what the left hand is doing. Ministers become overwhelmed with the many various pieces of ministry. When this happens the church becomes fragmented and no longer operates as a church family.

One saint by the name of JoAnn shared the following about her church with me:

> As I sit here with our church bulletin I see that one column is full of programs involving women—about five groups. The next column is mostly senior activities, then children, youth, on and on. Many groups trying to reach all ages and interests.
>
> All these groups [and] two worship services mean that we belong, or attend, the same church but we don't know each other. I personally don't know who is single, who is divorced, whose husband is deployed, who has only one car or no car and needs transportation, who is suffering depression, who has a sick child and could use a break, and yet my calendar is full. So how can we minister better than we are doing now?
>
> Are we, the church, failing certain people groups? We tend to minister to the properly dressed, friendly, educated, pretty people who are

able to reciprocate our kindness and friendship. "What would Jesus do?" "When I was hungry . . .When I was sick . . . When . . ."

Are we focusing on entertainment more than worship? Are we really loving as we try to teach? Are we teaching by script only or showing by example?

This is a fragmented church. There doesn't seem to be much connection between the children, the youth, the women, and other ministries. This appears to be a program-based church that has let things get out of control. You can read that JoAnn's heart is hurting for her church.

Sometimes church leaders get so used to the way they've always done programs that they don't see beyond the walls of their church. Kenny Conley says it best: "I've found that the longer I've followed Christ, the easier it is to become institutionalized. We surround ourselves with people who think like we do, act like we do, and believe like we do."[2]

What Is Family Ministry?

Currently family ministry is the buzzword among many church leaders. You can find several books on the subject of family ministry, and for now the definition of family ministry appears to be broad with many variations. One can hear the term *family ministry* being thrown around at almost every major religious conference.

In order to determine the structure of family ministry for your church, it is important for you to develop an organizational and missional strategy based on what scripture says. Some churches are slowly shutting down some of their programs and concentrating on ministries that impact the next generation. There is article after article about teens who leave the church once they graduate high school. Churches that adopt the idea for family ministry are concerned about the next generation.

For some churches family ministry means bringing cohesiveness to families. The church leadership works to pull families together in an organized fashion so that families are encouraged to be a family at church and at home. Parents are encouraged to lead in the spiritual formation of their children at home instead of leaving it up to the church.

Family ministry means:

- answering the question, "If children are born into our church and progress from infancy to adulthood, how should their faith development look?";
- partnering with the parents to equip them and encourage them to pass on their faith to their children and to the next generation; and
- providing opportunities for families to minister together.

Christine Yount Jones in an article titled "Trend Quakes" says,

> Increasing numbers of churches are strategically hiring a Family Ministry staff person and reorganizing their entire birth-through-high-school ministry under the umbrella of Family Ministry. Each age-specific ministry area plans, coordinates, schedules, communicates, and prays so everything they do supports and equips families. . . . Family Ministry is a way to bring the generations together. We are recognizing that by dividing our ministries exclusively by ages and stages (children, youth, young adult, middle adult, and older adults), we contribute to the fragmentation of families.[3]

Creating a family ministry doesn't mean you have to start all over. Take what you have and make it make sense. Develop your church's strategy so that all of the kids in your church are developing into disciples and growing in Christ. Work with the parents and equip them to bring the faith walk into their homes.

Family Ministry in a Small Church

At a small rural church in North Carolina that was struggling with revamping the mind-set of church members and moving more toward family ministry, Pastor Joey Chafton of Oak Grove Baptist Church, Youngsville, North Carolina, reported:

As a new pastor I am simply trying to redeem what we have in place and gently push towards a healthier model. So specifically with our men's breakfast we are encouraging all ages, six through eighty-five years of age, to join us for breakfast and a time studying the word. It's a pretty simple set up as we encourage a Titus 2 type of model—older and younger men challenging and encouraging one another.

As a whole I think a family-ministry–based church is created by putting the emphasis on the fathers leading and shepherding their families at home. Healthy homes equal healthy churches. Even in our children and youth ministries, we want one of our focuses to be on equipping the families to better serve the Lord. Discipleship of young people shouldn't be outsourced to a particular ministry of the church but begin in the home. So the more we can reduce age segregation and emphasize a family and Titus 2 model the healthier (and more biblical) we will be.

From another church we learn from Pastor Tom Ravan, First Baptist Church of Bessemer City, North Carolina, what family ministry looks like to him. I served under Pastor Tom at another church, and since I know him personally, I felt comfortable enough to interview him with specific questions. I had been impressed with how entire families came out to host community events. Little kids from one family worked alongside grandmas from another family. Teens worked, and we all enjoyed fellowship together as an intergenerational community. The experience always reminded me of what the New Testament church might have looked like.

My Questions to Pastor Tom

Linda: How did you come to develop the idea of setting up a booth at some of the community events?

Pastor Tom: I just wanted to meet people where they were. These events were large gatherings of people, so they provided good opportunities for us to get the name of Jesus outside the church walls. These included having booths set up at Tar River Festival, Youngsville Town Festival, and Meet in the Street at Wake Forest Town Festival.

Linda: What are some family-type events you are doing in your church now?

Pastor Tom: At the church we are at now, our town's festival is called Down Home Days. We will have a booth with balloon animals, popcorn, snow cones, take prayer requests, and give away a grill or a yard swing. Just as before, we will have all ages working the booth, and my daughter and I will be making the balloon animals. The key is to look to build relationships while we make balloon animals and while people fill out registration forms for giveaways, looking for opportunities to minister.

Linda: What does family ministry look like to you personally?

Pastor Tom: The big picture is we reach and minister to the whole family (all ages) not just pigeonholing based on job description. I try to plan events that have families in mind so that all can participate together. For me, it means I spend time with and love little ones as well as senior adults. It means when I plan a worship service, the music should be blended with the understanding that our congregation reaches all ages and preferences.

Segmented Family Ministry

Let's take a few minutes to use women's ministries as an example of how program-based classes can default to merely activities in a church building. It doesn't have to be women's ministry; it could be any ministry that separates the family.

The following is a sample of one week of women's classes in an average church:

1. Sunday morning women's-only Bible study

2. Midweek small group book study (women only)

3. Thursday scrapbook class (or any class about a hobby)

4. Friday mother's day out (could be in the evening or during the day)

5. Saturday morning training (this might be training for VBS, once a month study, and so on)

In one week it is possible for the mother to be involved in a women's-only group several times. I'm not saying any of these groups are wrong, but when any mother attends four or five women's-only groups within a week, when is she going to be involved as part of a family at church?

The children may not even go to the worship service with their parents because they are in a children's class or a youth group while the parents are in the service. Couple all of this with the fact that most children are involved in several afterschool activities. Many evenings the family doesn't sit down to eat together. It is possible that the majority of families in our country don't sit down for a family meal for weeks.

- When is the family a family?
- When are the children learning about a faith walk?
- When are the children being exposed to biblical standards?
- When is the family praying together?

Instead of several women's classes or groups, as my friend JoAnn shared was happening in her church, what if those classes turned into how to teach the women to disciple their children?

What if a little organization took place in JoAnn's church and mind-sets were changed to bring unity to the many programs?

- Perhaps for one of the women's Bible study groups the women brought their daughters along with them.

- The older women could show up in order to support, mentor, and share with the younger women and their daughters.
- For the men's Bible study group, they could bring their sons. If a boy didn't have a father in the church, one of the men could adopt him for these sessions, and the same for the women and young girls.

It might be possible to create a functioning church family where

- significant relationships are formed;
- church members know who is sick and needs help;
- others know whose husband has been deployed and needs prayer;
- even if there are two separate worship services, everyone feels like they belong to the same church family;
- there is a central place or way to convey prayer requests;
- when prayers are answered, people share;
- testimonies of God's grace and mercy are shared regularly; and
- family becomes family.

When you stop and think about it, many church families are like the families in our world today—running to and fro, trying to accommodate the children and all their activities. No one in the family is connecting on a heart level. Everyone in the family does his or her own thing. The family never comes together for a family meal during the week. Instead of the church imitating the worldly family, the church family can be the model for the worldly families. What might happen if we concentrated on turning the hearts of the parents toward the hearts of the children and the children toward the hearts of their parents like it says in Malachi in the Old Testament?

> He will turn the hearts of the parents to their children, and the hearts of the children to their parents; or else I will come and strike the land with total destruction. (Malachi 4:6)

Throughout the Old Testament, God told the people to teach their children. He told them to pass rituals and experiences down to their children. Over and over he had them create monuments that would stand to remind them of God's mercy and his protection and had them share the stories with their children. The New Testament starts with the genealogy of Christ and the birth of God's son. The concept of family begins the New Testament. In the New Testament, God gives us his son. Do you think God might sanction the family?

Some Observations from My Point of View

- The majority of teens who were raised in church are leaving the church after high school and not returning. This means the message of the gospel will more than likely not be transferred to the next generation in what was once a churched family.
- Many children are not being exposed to a Christian lifestyle.
- More and more couples are cohabiting instead of marrying. Most are not attending church, so their children are not being exposed to the local church.

I like how David Olson words the situation in his book *The American Church in Crisis*:

> The ongoing downturn in church attendance this millennium is partially related to external cultural changes. Many of the people in the emerging culture do not share the philosophical assumptions of 50-year-old churches or even of churches that are just 20 years old. Largely unaware of these changes, many churches continue to operate in the models and mentalities that no longer resonate with our culture.[4]

What about Fractured Families in Family Ministry?

You may be wondering how turning toward family ministry would help the single parent, the single adult, the boomer group, and other different kinds of families. All of the family types we've talked about in this book could benefit from a church that is family-ministry oriented. It might mean the family minister would oversee and coordinate various ministries to bring a sense of unity to the church family. In addition to helping families build family connections at home, this person pulls together support ministries, such as grief recovery and divorce support groups, to fit into the overall ministry plan. Many people in support groups simply fall away from the church after they complete their respective program. No planning or forethought has taken place to help these people know what to do, where they fit, or how to assimilate into the church family.

A church that is family oriented might start with a thirteen-week divorce recovery program for people who have experienced a divorce. After the person completed the class, depending on age and his or her situation, he or she could be introduced to leaders in other ministry areas. An older divorced grandmother could be encouraged to attend a class where other women close to her age are meeting for Bible study.

Single parents could be encouraged to attend a "single and parenting" Sunday morning class. This class could encourage them in their faith walk. It could take them to stories in the Bible about single parents. The lessons could help them learn how to parent their children alone. They would learn they are not alone in their parenting journey. Gradually, and after the initial shock of parenting alone wore off, they could be encouraged to participate in other family-type events in the church. They could be paired up with an older couple who could serve as grandparents for children whose own grandparents are far away. They could be introduced to how to do family worship in their single-parent home.

Many single parents need help parenting, and they need to show their children what a two-parent family looks like. But how they can they do that when they are only a one-parent family? After my divorce I was overwhelmed. My parenting was shelved while I tried to recover. It was hard to muster the energy to even go to church on Sunday. To be honest, if I hadn't been the church pianist I probably wouldn't have made it many Sundays. I was floundering in my Christian walk. And back in the 1980s there were no divorce recovery groups. The Lord placed two families in front of my children. For my daughter it was a family that lived down the street from us. Her best friend lived in this family. This dad took my daughter under his wing. She spent nights and weekends with them. My son also had a best friend at church. This family brought my son into the folds of their family during the time my son was in elementary school. He spent holidays with them. They celebrated birthdays together. He saw this family worship together at church.

All people groups need family. All family types need church family. Today I know many children who see me as a substitute grandparent. My children are grown and live far away from me. I've remarried, and my husband and I still need family. We develop relationships with the hurting in our midst. We connect on a heart level. The Lord continues to bring single-parent families my way and together we create family.

Defining Family Ministry

Most of the experts promoting family ministry use the following scriptures:

Deuteronomy 6:5-9: Love the LORD your God with all your heart and with all your soul and with all your strength. These commandments that I give you today are to be on your hearts. Impress them on your children. Talk about them when you sit at home and when you walk along the road, when you lie down and when you get up. Tie them as symbols on your hands and bind them on your foreheads. Write them on the doorframes of your houses and on your gates.

Matthew 28:18-20: Then Jesus came to them and said, "All authority in heaven and on earth has been given to me. Therefore go and make disciples of all nations, baptizing them in the name of the Father and of the Son and of the Holy Spirit, and teaching them to obey everything I have commanded you. And surely I am with you always, to the very end of the age."

I like to add another scripture:

Deuteronomy 6:20-21: In the future, when your son asks you, "What is the meaning of the stipulations, decrees and laws of the LORD our God has commanded you?" tell him . . ."

It doesn't say when your neighbor asks or when the government asks or when your friend asks. It says, "When your son asks."

Wayne Stocks, a children's minister in Ohio, touts, "The church is one of the few intergenerational places of community left in society. The role of grandparents, church members, and youth ministers can be pivotal in the faith development of a child of divorce."[5]

In an article I wrote for the Family Scholars Symposium Series, "Does the Shape of Family Shape Faith?" I address the question of how does a church, which focuses on traditional family ministry, minister to the child of divorce? This seems to be the question many churches are wrestling with as they try to define exactly what family ministry looks like. Divorcing families have indeed changed the landscape of what families look like within the church.

When I was invited to contribute to the Family Scholars Symposium response to the "Does the Shape of Families Shape Faith?" report, I wrote:

> In 43 years of ministering to children of divorce, I have personally observed many of the issues researched in the report. I'm beginning to think it is not so much the "shape" of family, while that has a lot to do with influencing children's faith, but it is the shape of the church surrounding the family.
>
> In my observation, many divorcing parents who are emotionally absent, in shock, or spend hours working to support their family, may not have the physical energy to take their children to church. If they take them to church they may not have the spiritual stamina to disciple their children in the home. . . .
>
> Churches and understanding leaders can bridge the gap between the child and their relationship with a heavenly Father by coming alongside the child. A church can replicate a loving family who can step up to the plate to assist and co-partner with the single parent to provide spiritual teaching and training to the children.[6]

Did you pick up on the phrase "it is the shape of the church surrounding the family"? I believe this to be true in every community where churches are trying to build their congregations, attract families, and connect all with serving a risen Savior.

Experts Speak

Dick Gruber likes to address the idea of families serving together in ministry. In the book *Collaborate Family + Church*, Dick says, "If you're truly sold on training children up in the way they should go, you must consider the endless possibilities when involving families together in ministry."[7] Reggie Joiner is founder and CEO of the re-Think Group and Orange, a nonprofit organization providing resources and training to help churches maximize their influence on the spiritual growth of the next generation.[8] He has also authored the book *Think Orange*.[9] Andy Stanley says, "*Think Orange* is not just another model or formula. It's a paradigm shift. It is a brand-new approach to capturing the hearts and imaginations of this generation's parent and kids."[10] Reggie believes family-friendly churches need to develop a strategic plan for families that is led by an integrated team. He thinks family ministry is not just another program but an intentional system that is thought through.

If you'd like to read more than fifty ministers' takes on family ministry, see the "Family Ministry Blog Tour Posts."[11] Whether you are the Reggie Joiners of the megachurch world or the Tom Ravans of the small to midsize church, you can do family ministry. What family ministry looks like to you and your church is up to you. If what you are currently doing is meeting the needs of your community, and you are bringing in the lost on a regular basis, kudos to you. The Kingdom needs more churches like yours.

The Church of the New Testament

When you think about it, the church is back where it was after the death of our Savior. From a few disciples the word began to spread. Believers met wherever they could to worship and learn about the Savior. The Holy Spirit met them in all kinds of places and locations. Many suffered even to the point of death so the word could be spread. And here we are today, struggling again for the sake of Christ to win a lost world to him. Perhaps we need to go back and learn from the New Testament church.

I think Eric Wallace in his book *Uniting Church and Home* sums it up best:

> The church should be the champion of the family since it is the institution designed by God to nurture and care for families. Despite its well-intentioned efforts, modern ministry has done very little to help strengthen families. In fact, much ministry has had the opposite effect. Family confusion and dysfunction is as great in Christian families as it is in non-Christian families. Perhaps we can best measure how the church has failed by looking at the future generation. Are youth today ready to take over leadership of the church tomorrow?[12]

Suggested Resources

D6 Conference. http://d6conference.com/. D6 conference is a conference to champion a movement of parents who connect with their kids spiritually to transfer their faith based upon the principles of Deuteronomy 6:5-7.

The following sites are operated by the reThink Group and include detailed information about new concepts in family ministry:

- 252 Basics. www.252basics.org. Explanation about 252 basics.
- Amber Sky Records. www.amberskyrecords.com. Offers songs, videos, charts, and more items to help churches as they use the Orange curriculum.
- Camp KidJam. www.campkidjam.com. Teaches kids how to grow together in faith.
- "First Look." Orange. www.myfirstlook.org. Introduction to Orange philosophy.
- MarriedPeople. www.marriedpeople.org. Helpful tips to help churches help marriages.

- Orange. www.whatisorange.org. This site opens the door to children's ministry curriculum and other Orange curriculum ideas.
- Orange Conference. www.theorangeconference.com. Explains in detail about what one can glean from attending the Orange conference along with the many conference leaders and speakers.
- Orange Leaders. www.orangeleaders.com. Provides updated information for orange leaders.

Visionary Family Ministries. http://visionaryfam.com/.

Chapter 9

Electronic Steeples

Social Media and the Digital World

We will tell the next generation
the praiseworthy deeds of the LORD,
his power, and the wonders he has done.

—Psalm 78:4

Years ago church steeples stood tall in communities. Everyone knew the building with a steeple was a church. In our world today, social media is becoming the electronic steeple. How tall is your electronic steeple? Is it attracting the families in your community? Visibility of your church must be strong and widespread in many different ways. Families have many activities competing for church attendance. Ministers and church leaders need to research the best way to make it convenient for families to find and learn more about their church.

Experts say young families and young people under thirty will go to the Internet first to look for a church. However, our world is changing rapidly since the introduction of social media and the Internet. More and more people of all ages are going to the Internet to find answers. Those answers include finding a church as well as finding answers to life problems or seeking help during a crisis. People are looking for relational ministries where they can connect and where they matter.

The Fast-Moving Digital World

The digital world is moving rapidly, faster than anyone over thirty years of age could ever have imagined. I hesitated writing this chapter because some of the information in this chapter will more than likely be out-of-date by the time the book is published. However, I believe there is still a lot we can learn, and we can even benefit from the early mistakes many churches made in using the Internet and social media.

If your church hasn't jumped on the digital bandwagon, you might want to seriously consider it. Albert Mohler says, "If you are not present on the Internet, you simply do not exist, as far as anyone under thirty is concerned. . . . [The digital world] is one of the most important arenas of leadership our generation will ever experience. If you are satisfied to lead from the past, stay out of the digital world. If you want to influence the future, brace yourself and get in the fast lane."[1] The momentum in the digital world for communication is astounding. Now when a news event happens, videos and pictures along with personal accounts of the event flood the media. Many times people on Twitter broadcast a crisis before any national news media is privy to it. Information is disseminated globally faster than one can make a phone call. People around the world used to march in protest of something and raise their fists. Now they gather around, raise their smartphones, and click. Currently the Internet, social media, and smartphones are the communication tools. Who knows what there will be in five, ten years? E-mail has already gone by the wayside for the younger generation. They no longer send e-mails, and phone calls are passé. Communication and connections are done via text. Personal computers are also disappearing as smaller handheld devices are cropping up.

When a pastor says, "Pull out your Bible," many people pull out their smartphone or tablet to look up the scriptures. Savvy congregants will also hold a minister accountable by looking up facts and stories online while he or she is still preaching. We are learning that technology is changing how we learn. The younger population will not wait around for elders in a church to make decisions about the use of technology. This group will vote with their feet—they will walk out the back door. If you don't have an active and up-to-date website, the younger generation, the boomer generation, and all those in between will not find you in the first place.

New to a Community

When I found out we were moving to Florida to help my son-in-law care for my three grandsons while my daughter was deployed to Afghanistan, the first thing I did was go to the Internet and look at all the churches that were in the area where we were going to be living. I have to say that was frustrating in many ways. The next thing I searched out was the area itself. To give you an idea of what a new person or family moving into your area might look for, here is what I was looking to find:

- I wanted to see what the community offered: what restaurants were nearby, what community events were held—in general what the area was like. On the community calendar I looked to see what churches had their events posted.
- I then checked out my grandsons' schools.
- Since my daughter was leaving in the summer, I wanted to find out what kind of summer activities were available for boys who were three, eight, and almost thirteen years old.
- The first place I looked was the website of the church the boys attended:
    1. I looked for information on their Vacation Bible School.
    2. I checked to see if there were any summer camps available for the older boys.
    3. I searched to see what was available for the pre-schooler on Sundays and other times we might want to attend an event.

4. I searched for when church services began on Sundays.

5. I checked midweek activities for adults.

6. I looked for a Bible study for older couples or women's and men's Bible studies.

7. I searched for what was available to single parents, people divorcing, or those facing grief because of a death.

8. Since this church was in an area heavily populated by military bases, I looked for activities for military families.

9. I wanted information about each pastor: his or her degrees, experience, and role at the church.

10. I also wanted to find out the distance from my daughter's house to the church.

11. I wanted the physical address of the church as well as the phone number of the church and e-mail addresses of the staff.

FYI – not once did I look at a phone book or the yellow pages. This is a brave new world.

Church Websites and Common Mistakes

While living in North Carolina, I had the privilege of working as a consultant for Church Initiative, where part of my job was to connect with churches and view church websites—*hundreds* of church websites.[2] I think one of the most frustrating parts of the day was trying to decipher information on these websites. Here are the things that bothered me most about some of these websites, and I'd venture to say most people searching for information on your church would feel the same way:

1. The site has a background that is too dark and uses fonts in dark colors, like gray or brown.

2. The site starts up with music and cutesy graphics. Most people will skip the music and graphics because they want to get to the meat of the information.

3. The site loads up s-l-o-w-l-y! I can't tell you how many times I have sat drumming my fingers on the desk waiting for a site to load. If I were a newcomer looking for a church, I would have clicked off right away.

4. The name of the church is not on every page.

5. There is no physical address that is easy to find on the site.

6. The site doesn't have a map or a place to click where a person can put in his or her address and pull up a map with driving instructions to your church.

7. There is no contact name or the contact just says "Ken." Who is "Ken"?

8. There is no phone number or e-mail address, or they are hard to find. People don't want to spend time looking for something that should be readily available.

9. Finding information about classes and ministries is difficult to locate.

10. The site is not current or up-to-date. It is March and the information on Christmas cantata is still posted on the front page.

A few years ago many churches threw together websites without much thought given to them. They mostly contained basic information about staff members and a schedule of services. Today your website has replaced your church's front door and steeple, so it is important to put much thought into developing your website. You can do a Google search by putting in "developing a church website" and come up with many companies and individuals who will assist your church.

For most small or midsize churches, it might be prudent to invest in a web designer. Doing this can actually save money in the long run. If you have someone in your church who can work with the designer, more than likely the designer can teach that person how to update your site regularly. Go online and see what websites for churches in your area look like.

It is amazing that some of the big-name churches have convoluted websites. They are hard to navigate. They are so full of graphics and videos that one can get lost just trying to research the church. Think through carefully the purpose of your website—what do you want to convey to the newcomer? What do you want her or him to know about your church?

When designing the site make sure to have a prominent navigation bar. This can be at the top or on the side, but wherever it is, it needs to be visible when one first looks at your site. Without a good navigation bar it is like being lost in a foreign land without a good map. The navigation bar needs to be on every page. A navigation bar needs to include the following pages:

- Home—you might have a picture of your church on the home page. Post a scripture and something that says, "Welcome to our church." Type only about 350 words on the home page, if that many. The home page should be a place to land and quickly reflect—this is the place I want to know more about.
- About—the about page can be where you put detailed information about your church. You can post pictures of people involved in various ministries or information about the year your church was founded. This is the place you can post names, biographies, and pictures of the church staff.
- Contact—the contact page can be simple, with a place to post the name of a contact person along with an e-mail address and church phone number. Some churches allow a newcomer to type an e-mail right on the page and click "send."

- Welcome—I like a welcome page. On this page there can be a welcoming message that sounds friendly and upbeat. You can include your church's goals, mission, or vision statement. Provide a form much like a visitor form a person would fill out during a worship service. One church site I visited recently said something like, "The ministries of the church are designed to enrich and equip your life," on the welcome page. Now that is something that would make me want to know more about this church.

- Ministries—this is a place to list all of the ministries your church provides, with links to learn more about each ministry. Some churches post the name and contact information of the person to contact to learn more. Drop-down boxes, where you hover over the word *ministry* and the ministries show up, are okay, but many people prefer to be able to click on the word *ministry* and have all the ministries of the church show up on the ministry page. A person can then click on the ministry they want to learn more about. When one clicks on a particular ministry, it is good to be able to view a short video or pictures of people actually doing ministry.

- Calendar—some churches post a calendar of events. I've seen churches use an actual monthly calendar; this makes it clear and concise. Be sure not to overwhelm visitors with too many activities or comments. A long list of events going down the page will not be attractive to visitors.

- Church news—post exciting news about your church or any news articles that have been in the local paper or online.

- Schedules—always have the service times posted in a prominent place. I've seen several church websites where the main service times were posted at the bottom of each page.

- Giving—make it easy for church members and visitors to give to your church by providing a place online to make their donations. Use a system that tracks the giving so at the end of the year a document detailing contributions can be sent via e-mail to each person or family.

- FAQ—a frequently asked questions section is a relatively new concept I've seen a few times. It does make sense in our world of unchurched visitors. Think how scary it might be to enter a strange new world and not know the customs, dress requirements, or even the language. Put everything in this section you think a visitor might want to know:

1. How do most of your congregants dress: casual, business casual, formal?

2. What words does your church use that are particular to your church—*baptism, Communion, sacraments?* Give a definition of these terms.

3. How does one donate, via an offering plate that is passed, drop box, online?

4. What are the "rules" for taking Communion?

5. How does your church handle singing? Is it okay to clap one's hands or raise hands? Are words on a screen or are people expected to use hymnbooks? Or is the music traditional?

6. Are children allowed to worship in the service with their parents or does your church provide a children's worship service?

7. Is there a nursery for infants and toddlers? Is it okay for a nursing mom to bring her baby to the worship service with her?

8. What about teenagers? Do they have a separate service?

What to Do When Creating Your Church's Website

- Limit text on each page to no more than five hundred words.
- Use headings and bullet points when writing more than a couple of sentences.
- Make the page readable for a quick scan.
- Update the site regularly. For most churches, that will be weekly.
- Create a website that is easy to read and navigate.

Remember

- Small fonts make reading difficult for many older people.
- Just because an infographic looks good to you doesn't mean that it belongs on your site.
- Cute videos may impress some church staff, but they may deter a visitor.
- Posting videos of your trip to Belize or Guatemala without an explanation makes no sense to visitors.
- Weird music makes people click off your site quickly.
- If website visitors can directly e-mail the church, please check that e-mail account daily.

Churches can take a page out of the business world: the very life of the business depends on the website. Business owners know that first impressions of a website influence a person's judgment of the company's credibility and the customer's buying decisions.

What is your church's website selling? Don't we want our church website to impress a visitor so that he or she will want to attend our church? Think about what your church is selling—music, sermons, activities, relationships, salvation?

Research from the Business World

- A clean, professional, and fast-loading site can ensure that your first impression will be a good one.
- Make sure your website loads quickly on a mobile device. Some business experts say that if your site doesn't load in five seconds on a mobile device you will lose approximately 74 percent of your audience. Mobile devices are quickly outpacing desktop browsing. Do not use Flash; keep photos and videos to a minimum.[3]
- Prime real estate on sites is the top right-hand corner. Put the most important information you want people to see in that spot.
- First impressions can influence subsequent judgments of website credibility and buying decisions.
- Things that were found to harm credibility were

  - difficult navigation,
  - typographic errors,
  - broken links,
  - stale content, and
  - poor design (creates mistrust).

- A good layout is of utmost importance.
- Content needs to be organized, not randomly thrown on your site.
- According to Missouri University of Science and Technology you've got 2.6 seconds to make that important first impression on your website visitors. That's how long it takes them to settle on the most captivating element of your site.[4] However, it appears that first opinions of your site, and thus your church, are formed in milliseconds—0.05 seconds.

Outreach to your community via the Internet will bring people to your church. As you choose programs and ministries for your church, make sure the organization producing the product provides your church with suggestions or a means to promote it digitally. A good example of outreach via a ministry is Church Initiative, the organization that produces "point of pain" ministries such as DivorceCare, GriefShare, DC4K (DivorceCare for Kids), and other programs for people in crisis. They provide a Find-a-Group platform. On the Find-a-Group page, visitors can put in their zip code, click, and do up to a one-hundred-mile search to see which churches in their area provide one of these ministries.

Steve Grissom, the founder and president of Church Initiative, reported:

> Our Find-a-Group online search tool is the single most visited section of our websites. Hurting people want quick information on how to find help, and this technology lets them generate an immediate list of DivorceCare, DC4K, GriefShare, or Single & Parenting groups meeting nearby them. There is no question our growth would have been much slower without the search capability.
>
> Many local churches tell us that the Find-a-Group search tool is the most effective way they have of promoting their groups. It facilitates outreach into their communities.

How the Digital World Assists Churches in Spreading the Word

- Effective outreach—church staff and outreach teams used to go out and physically visit the people who had attended their church for the first time. With our busy world, research shows most visitors to a church don't want a physical visit. More than likely you wouldn't find them home anyway. In-the-know churches have realized they can do outreach via social media.
- New tools—Many pastors no longer use handwritten or typed sermon notes but devices such as an iPad. Charles Stone has

a great booklet on how to use your iPad to become a better leader.[5] Charles gives some good advice about apps for you to preach from and tips on how to prepare and preach a sermon using an iPad.

- Live streaming—the sermon on Sunday morning can be made available to shut-ins in your church or to people on the other side of the world. I've known people who have tuned into a live stream of a service to "test out" the minister before they moved to a new area. A word of caution on live streaming an entire service—make sure you have permission to live stream music that is copyright protected. Just because a song is on YouTube doesn't give you permission to broadcast it.

  Many conferences are now live streaming main conference speakers. To give you an idea of numbers and how live streaming can reach thousands, consider the 2013 Chick-fil-a Leadercast event in Atlanta.[6] Approximately five thousand attended the live event while another 115,000 watched via satellite in 750 locations around the world.

- E-mail—even though e-mail has lost its appeal to the younger generation, many ministers and church leaders still use it as an effective means of communication. Some churches will use e-mail as the first form of communication for visitors. Announcements can be made via e-mail. Sunday's bulletin can be e-mailed a few days in advance of Sunday's service. Invitations to various events can be e-mailed.

- Blogosphere—blogs are growing at such a rapid pace it is difficult to keep up. Ministers can use blogs to teach and train their congregants. You can post up-and-coming sermons and scriptures. As a minister you can blog about personal events in your life so your congregants feel a relational connection to you.

- Apps—churches are making use of apps to present media to their congregants in easy-to-use mobile formats. Churches use them for podcasts, for prayer walls, for comment walls, for small groups or group support workbooks, and to communicate messages—the applications seem to be limited only by one's imagination. If you want to attract the under-thirty group, which is where you'll find many young families, and keep them coming to your church, use apps. This group uses apps in abundance. If you are concerned about how to create apps, there are several professional groups that will create an app for your specific need.

- Video conferencing—church leaders are finding it difficult to conduct face-to-face meetings, so they are turning to online meetings. Some experts will tell you to stop holding so many meetings where everyone has to be physically present. More than likely you will have several people not able to attend.

  Use one of the new digital methods to have those meetings. Todd McKeever explains on his site[7] the advantages of using Skype[8] or Live Minutes.[9] Todd says he estimates that with these two tools he conducts 70 percent of his meetings with his children's ministry teams online. He connects better with all the leaders, and he also says it allows him to have more time at home with the family. In the same blog post Todd says Live Minutes "provides a place to add Excel, Word, PDF type documents and work on them together in real time. You can add more documents during the video call as well and then when it is all done everyone can get a recording and PDF of the video meeting." While our world seems to be shrinking, and with so many people pulling away from Christianity, churches that take full advantage of the new digital age will be blessed by reaching many for the kingdom of God.

Social Media

There are many social network platforms. Currently Facebook, Twitter, and Pinterest seem to be the top contenders. Matt McKee, CEO of ROAR,[10] conducted a "Social Media in Church Survey."[11] He discovered the platforms churches use most and the approximate percentage of these platforms:

- Facebook—99 percent
- Twitter—almost 80 percent
- Blogs—43 percent
- Instagram—14 percent
- Pinterest—14 percent

I have to say the 14 percent use of Pinterest surprised me, because it seems like almost every church children's leader that I know uses Pinterest. Perhaps the reason I see so much use of Pinterest is because the posts are coming from children's leaders who are volunteers and who are mostly parents, not church leaders, posting activities, projects, and pictures. I think we'll see more social networks like Pinterest popping up in the future.

Social Media Tips

Social media can help churches reach more people in their communities. It can help you form deeper connections and relationships with people in your church and with people in your community. Make no mistake, social media allows you to interact in a fast-paced world.

Facebook

Currently Facebook is the most popular of the social media venues. Facebook is open to everyone. If your church doesn't have at least one Facebook page, it is easy to get started. If you are a little nervous about how to get started, find a trustworthy teenager in your church who can help you.

There are different types of pages. There are personal pages, where you have your own personal profile. Your church can use group pages or fan pages. Take some time to learn about each kind. Some group pages are open, meaning anyone can see the group, who is in it, and what members post. There are closed groups, where anyone can see the group and who's in it but only members can see posts. Then there is the secret group, where only members see the group, who's in it, and what members post.

Matt McKee advises churches in his book *Be Social: The Social Media Handbook for Churches* to create a community page for church membership.[12] With the advent of smartphones, photographs of church events can be uploaded before the event is over. Church members can be tagged in pictures, and events can be shared among church members.

For some churches it is best for each ministry to have its own page in addition to the community church members' page. Many children's ministers and youth ministers make wise use of this venue. On public pages, parents and volunteers can keep up with the latest happenings in the ministry. Announcements can be made. One church I know posts the up-and-coming scriptures for Sunday. The entire family knows in advance what the message is going to be.

A word of caution—do not post pictures of children on public pages. Create a private children's ministry page to post pictures of children at church, in activities, and at events.

How to create a Facebook fan page for your ministry:

1. Go to www.Facebook.com/pages/create.php

2. Click on "Company, Organization or Institution"

3. Click the drop-down box, and select "Church/Religious Organization"

4. Put in the name of what you want to call your Facebook page

5. Check the box agreeing to the Facebook pages terms

6. Click "Get Started"

7. Follow all the instructions

I have a personal Facebook page. I love connecting with ministers and people all over the world. Some of the DC4K (DivorceCare for Kids) leaders in other countries have friended me. We pray for one another, for our ministries, and for our families. People who have come to training events I've done are now my friends on Facebook. Now one of the most exciting parts of attending a ministry conference is meeting face-to-face with friends on Facebook. I can't wait to meet up in heaven with so many of God's wonderful servants. Because of some of the groups I've joined, I gain access to a lot of research, and I learn a lot from articles and blogs posted on Facebook. I actually do quite a bit of ministry work via Facebook. It is not unusual to hear from a pastor in another state who is struggling with a single parent. I do a lot of single-parent coaching via Facebook.

Twitter

Second in the running for social media is Twitter. Twitter is quickly gaining momentum with the younger crowd. On Twitter, messages are made up of 140 characters. I try to make my messages even shorter than that so I can add a hashtag (#) to them. A hashtag draws certain people or groups to your message. When I post a message about the child of divorce, I use the hashtag #KidMin.

Twitter is fairly easy to get started using. To create a Twitter account for your ministry go to www.twitter.com and follow the instructions.

Todd McKeever says that at his church they have used Twitter as an express way for some of their families to get checked in: "On the way to church they tweet us a direct message and we check them in and print their security tags off so that when they get to church they skip the lines at check-in."[13]

On Twitter you can share the following:

- A quotation
- Scriptures
- Cute stories
- Pictures
- Personal thoughts
- Encouragement
- Up-and-coming events
- Congratulations to people and children on their accomplishments
- Blog posts or news items

Whether you are posting on Facebook or Twitter, remember others will see your post. Complaints and criticisms have no place in these venues. Keep an eye on what your friends and family post on Facebook. I have friended many teens through the years. Some of their posts are not appropriate for younger children. One time a troubled teen posted an inappropriate post. Of course, it showed up on my page. I immediately posted a reply, "Hey, bub, if you want to stay my friend, you'll get this message off here!" I got an immediate apology back within seconds. The message was deleted. This young man lives in another state, but we stay connected on Facebook. You can also always hide inappropriate messages and even unfriend an individual, which I have also done.

Many ministers will have children as friends on Facebook. Even though children are not supposed to be on Facebook, they are. Be very cautious of what shows up on your page. Do not hesitate to unfriend anyone who is inappropriate. The great thing about social media for ministers, especially youth and children's ministers, is that it gives them an incredible opportunity to impact a child's life for the Kingdom. And it can happen daily too.

Technology Trends

Technology is shaping education systems around the world. Research shows that technology is rewiring the way we learn. Churches are going to have to keep up with the education system if they want to attract young families. We can learn from other groups, and the education system is already ahead of the religious community in this area. This doesn't mean that we have to turn worldly, but it does mean that churches are wise if they take cues from groups that have already developed their tools.

Any way you look at it, technology and digital learning will trickle down into the church's children and youth programs. There are several changes I see happening in children and youth ministries. First of all, practically every kid has a smartphone. Everything is done on the smartphone. Encourage kids to use their smartphones at church to look up scriptures. Create devotions or find online devotions and send them out to the kids' mobile devices. Kids can explore Bible lessons and research biblical truths online. Computer games and game-based learning are rampant. No longer will kids sit through a boring presentation on Sunday after being flooded with digitally-based learning during the week. Interactive learning is all the rage in schools. It needs to be that way in church also. E-books are quickly taking over. Schools are moving away from printed books, and church will begin to consider that option also. A lot of children have access to various mobile devices. Use this opportunity for God's glory.

Children and youth pastors who write their own curriculum will need to embrace a different set of skills. It is going to take program design and interactive skills to keep the kids' attention. More than likely smaller churches will have to bite the bullet, so to speak, and purchase ready-made ministry helps. Youth ministers will be expected to stay in touch with youth from the church. Most youth will expect to connect with the youth minister by smartphone or other mobile device on a regular basis. Youth ministries will also need to address and study moral principles in this fast-paced #geteverything-insecondsonline world. Youth today have many more temptations and avenues to express and become involved in inappropriate behavior such as viewing pornography. And they are doing it at younger and younger ages.

Want to Know More?

If you want to know more about digital platforms, programs, or exactly how to connect to the new digital age, contact a children's minister. The majority of these ministers grew up in the information age. They are screen junkies, and they make great use of these media to impact the kingdom of God. One incredible place to find and connect with children's ministers is CMConnect. (http://my.cmconnect .org). CMConnect is a social media of sorts for children's pastors. Michael Chanley, a children's minister, started it several years ago. When I joined it had just four hundred members, and today it has more than ten thousand. You can search for any digital device and you'll find a post, a discussion, a blog, or a video podcast about it on CMConnect.

Chapter 10

Making Worship Family Friendly

All the men of Judah stood before the LORD,
with their little ones, their wives, and their children.

—2 Chronicles 20:13 RSV

The Little Man

He was only three years old when he dressed himself in his favorite clothes, stuck a small notebook under his arm, and went to church. There was something odd about that small notebook stuck under his arm. It looked vaguely familiar, but I couldn't place it. He sat in between his Papa Bruce and me. He did his best to pay attention—drawing in his small notebook, looking around to see what other people were doing. He observed the adults and tried to act like them. After the service he grabbed his small notebook and under his arm it went. He walked down the aisle sticking his little short arm and hand out to anyone who would look his way. He said, "Welcome. Glad you are here," as he shook the hands of bewildered adults. Then it dawned on me why that small notebook under the arm looked familiar. It was exactly what his Papa Bruce did with his Bible. This little tyke acted and said exactly what his Papa Bruce had modeled for him. A grandfather and a three-year-old in worship together—what a precious time.

Worship services may very well be the last remnant of inter-generational gatherings in our world today. Christian churches that encourage family worship are places where children and youth can connect in a meaningful way with other generations while they learn about God and holiness. Family worship can strengthen bonds between youth and parents. It can serve to encourage sibling cohesiveness. Worship is a place for family.

There is a continual discussion going on in the children's- and youth-ministry world about allowing children to join in worship services. Some children's ministers feel children should not be in "big" church, while others believe children should be exposed to regular church services. As a matter of fact, it is probably the hottest debate going on among children's ministers.

This chapter is not meant to change your mind if you strongly believe children should not be included in the worship service. If having separate places for children during worship is working for you, continue what you are doing. However, if you already have family worship or if you are researching the idea of family worship, this chapter is for you. We've stated in other chapters that for the most part Christians are in a minority. In our country unchurched is the majority, so if you are thinking about attracting all kinds of families to your church, think about attracting the unchurched family, whether that is the two-parent family, the single-parent family, the blended family, the grandparent family, or any other family.

When you bring people in, keep the family unit before God and together in family worship. Families live in a disconnected world and, for many unchurched families, coming together in worship may be a new experience and one that will bring them closer together as a family unit.

Doing Church as a Single Parent

I was having a conversation with a children's pastor and the subject of family worship came up. I explained I felt it was important for single parents to sit with their children in the worship service. She said she thought single parents would want a break from their children. And since there was only one parent, there would be no one to help the single mom if the kids got out of control.

It dawned on me that unless you are a single parent or were raised in a single-parent household, you might not understand the significance of worshiping with your children. When I was a single parent, it was a time to come together as a family. I wanted my kids to sit with me because they were only there every other weekend. In other words, I only had them with me half the Sundays out of the year. I felt a sense of panic in teaching them Christian values and principles when I didn't have as much time as those in two-parent homes did. Worshiping together brought a sense of peace and unity to our family. And goodness knows single parents who have experienced a divorce need peace and a sense of unity brought into the home. Many Sundays one of the kids would snuggle up next to me and lay his or her head on my shoulder. They watched me pray intently for their father. They watched brothers and sisters in Christ come up and hug me before and after church. They heard people tell me that they were praying for me. For me, being at church with my kids was a special, intimate time.

Another single mom I met at a conference in California explained that she worked on consistently teaching her children not only to sit still but also to be still. She said they practiced all of the time. They practiced it in the grocery store, at the doctor's, and on the way to church. She said friends criticized her, but her comeback was, "If you don't teach your children to be quiet and still as children, how will they ever know how to be still before the Lord?" Even though she was in a church that separated children from the worship service, she took her kids with her and taught them to sit still before the Lord.

Lessons Learned from Children's Church

I've been in churches that have a short children's time in the front of the church. I've overheard adults say, "I get more out of the children's message than I do the sermon." It might be because the children's minister

- tells stories,
- uses visual props,
- employs word pictures,
- asks thought-provoking questions,
- explains how the scripture relates to life problems, and
- keeps the message short and sweet.

Rarely do you hear children's ministers ramble. If they do, they lose the children's attention. Children are very honest and forthright. They will get up and walk away, or they will just start talking in the middle of a sentence. What if we applied the standards above to sermons for the family?

From the Eyes of a Child

Making worship family friendly might mean you take a closer look at the worship life of your church. Look at it through the eyes of a child. Ask other ministers and church leaders what they think a child would see. Go in your sanctuary or worship center and get down on your knees and take a look around. What does the environment look like from a three- or four-foot level? If you are just starting to develop a family-friendly service, or if you have new families coming into the church, think about taking the children into your worship area during a weekday. Allow them to walk around and look at things.

When my daughter was deployed, most of the care of the three-year-old fell upon me. One evening after we moved into my daughter's house, I had to go to an extra choir rehearsal. Because it was an extra rehearsal, there was no childcare scheduled. I explained to the three-year-old that, since his dad was at the base and his Papa Bruce was working, he would have to go with me to the extra rehearsal. In preparation, we discussed the following differences:

- The place where we sat on Sunday morning would have no people in it.

- There were several questions and explanations why there would be no people in "that room."
- I told him he could come up and sit in the choir loft with me or he could choose to sit in one of the pews.
- I explained since the preacher would not be preaching and there would no people in the seats, we could take time for him to look at things.

When we got to the church we took a walk around the sanctuary:

- He stopped and touched different things.
- He went over to the keyboard and piano area, and I explained this was where the people that made the music sat and played these instruments.
- He walked up and down several aisles. Think how different this looked to a little body only about three feet high. He had only sat in one area toward the back, so this was all new to him.
- When we got ready to practice he came up on the stage, looked around, and then sat with the choir. He was surprised and said, "Nana, it's really different up here!"
- When he got tired of helping us sing he walked to the back of the church and, with the permission of the soundman, was able to go into the sound booth.

A funny thing happened after that experience. This little fellow took ownership of his church the next Sunday. He was so proud about all that he knew. He stood tall that Sunday and sang his little heart out during the service. He was relaxed and comfortable in the service.

Remember, if an unchurched family or family new to your denomination or church affiliation attends your church, the children may not be familiar with what it is like to attend your worship service. You might need to teach the parents how to prepare children for a worship service. This could be accomplished through a short video or DVD that each new parent would receive. Or you might put it on your website in a document form.

An Example of Family-Friendly Worship

About ten years ago my husband and I had been in North Carolina for a while, and we had visited many churches trying to determine where the Lord wanted us to serve. We had planned on visiting a church not too far from where we lived, when we saw a sign announcing they would be starting a new service. We were there the first morning that Rolesville Baptist in Rolesville, North Carolina, started their new Morning Glory service. This service was started, first of all, because they were out of space in the sanctuary; second, they had several young families requesting a family-friendly service. Jeffrey Pethel, the minister of Christian education, said families wanted a less formal space where they could bring their children to worship service with them.

Even though the church had conducted meetings and had researched starting this adventure for weeks before, the Morning Glory service was a work in progress. It was not a formal service held in their sanctuary but an informal service held in the family life center. It wasn't long before the church had to move to the gym because of the growing attendance at the Morning Glory service. Instead of a formal choir there was a praise team. The second week of the new service I joined the praise team as their keyboardist. I had a great place to serve and to observe the inner workings of developing a family-friendly worship experience.

From the very beginning there was no nursery available at the early service. Parents brought all ages of children into the service and continue to do so. Parents know their infants and toddlers are welcomed. Babies are held, put on blankets on the floor, or passed from person to person. When they cry, parents can walk to the back of the church or into the hallway to calm their infant. It is a matter-of-fact incident, and no one thinks anything about a parent walking to the back of the room.

Children are acknowledged as valuable contributors to the

church family. When there is a greeting time, children as well as older adults, teens, and all ages are greeted. Youth play instruments on the praise team. Youth contribute through singing solos, passing out bulletins, and providing other assistance the minister might need during the service. When the church has Communion, children are provided with a small bag of goldfish crackers. The church leaves it up to families to decide regarding Communion. The children who do not take Communion are told that they can eat their crackers when the adults take Communion. Pastor Jeff says he always tells the children at this time that God loves them and "so does your church family."

I have seen men and sons serve as ushers together. There is something special about playing an offertory and watching an eight- or nine-year-old boy walk alongside his dad who is passing offering plates. Pastor Jeff always has something in the back of the gym for the children to use during the service. Sometimes he makes use of children's church bulletins. Other times he provides color sheets that might have a Bible story on one side with a scripture and a place to color on the back. This facilitates a family Bible discussion at home. There are usually two or three options to choose from.

Connections That Form Lifelong Relationships

When we were serving at Rolesville Baptist, I always sat at the keyboard toward the front of the gym. Each Sunday Pastor Jeff had a short children's time. As the children walked toward Pastor Jeff, I was able to connect with many of these kids. It was not unusual for me to receive several colored pictures at the end of the service. Today, I still get pictures via Facebook that a child has colored during the service.

Before the service at Rolesville Baptist Church, the family life center is open and congregants can take part in a preservice meal. It is very informal with a breakfast buffet set up. Families sit together or can spread out and sit with other people. It is not unusual to see little children sitting with older adults. One can hear a lot of laughter and witness many hugs. The feeling of church family is intimate at the preservice time.

What Church Can Do

Make it obvious that children are welcomed throughout the entire church. At Sierra Vista United Methodist Church in San Angelo, Texas, children are valued. Children's artwork is displayed on the walls. They have water fountains close to the worship center. There is a cart with children's books and Bibles, crayons, paper, and other items to be used during the service.

In their pew pockets "there are words of assurance for visiting families, telling them not to worry about wiggly and giggly children and that the congregation is pleased to see families gathered together as they journey in faith."[1] They also provide rockers in the sanctuary, where parents can hold and soothe young children. In addition, children at Sierra Vista United Methodist Church serve as greeters and ushers and are involved in all parts of the service.

Make all parts of the worship experience family friendly. That means it is family friendly from the point of entrance, to the worship service, through the music, prayers, offerings, and sermon, to the closing benediction.

What Ushers Can Do

- Remember to shake the hands of the children as they enter the service.
- Offer to allow children and youth to help hand out bulletins or visitor cards.
- Encourage children and youth to serve with you and help congregants who are disabled or other people who might need help getting in and out of cars or walking down the aisle.
- Thank children and youth for their attendance.

What Worship Leaders Can Do

- Introduce a new praise song and repeat it for several weeks in a row before introducing another new song.

- Include an older hymn occasionally for the boomers and families who might have been out of church for years.
- Provide words on a PowerPoint presentation or put the page number of the songs in the bulletin.
- If possible, allow children to help lead the songs.
- Invite youth to play the drums, guitar, or other instruments to accompany the singing.

What Ministers Can Do

- When creating family-friendly sermons, think about preaching to the teenagers in your congregation. If you can hold their attention, you can probably hold the attention of the entire family. Teens don't understand doctrinal concepts or deep theological theories. They understand the here and now. Save the doctrinal lessons for small groups or for the times when youth meet together.
- Don't be fooled by people who think you should dumb down your message for the kids. People who think this way come across as condescending to the children. If you try this approach, more than likely you'll lose the interest of the children as well as the adults. Children need authentic worship. They need to see and feel your emotions. Children are likely to do what is modeled for them.
- Preach the gospel. Tell people how to accept Christ. Sometimes we forget that not everyone knows what to do, how to pray, or what to say when accepting Christ as God's son.
- Preach the word. Families need to hear what the Bible says about life. You may have to think about changing your approach, but never change the gospel.
- Preach short and concise messages. Brain research shows that our technical advances have rewired our brains. People's brains will listen in spurts.

- Change things up about every ten minutes, because that is how long you can keep the congregation's attention. Move to the other side of the platform. Raise your hand. Change the PowerPoint slide.
- Don't be afraid to ask people to join in. When I was a guest trainer at an event at a church in Texas, during the middle of the worship service the minister started singing. I mean out of the blue he started singing the song "Deep and Wide." The congregation didn't hesitate as they joined right in. Not only did he start singing the song, he also used the motions. Kids were excited, teens were bored but they sang anyway, and all the adults sang and joined in with the motions. I must have had a quizzical look on my face because the guy next to me leaned over and said, "He does this all the time. Just breaks out in song."

   I was invited back the next year and, sure enough, the minister broke out in song again. This time the words suddenly appeared on the screen. As soon as the song was over, without missing a beat, the minister continued his sermon. The song always fits the message. This minister keeps the attention of his people.
- Tell stories. People learn through stories. Our minds grab onto stories, the stories sink in and resonate with us, and then our minds absorb how we can use them in our own lives. Think Jesus and the parables.
- Since people also learn through word pictures, paint a scene to go along with the scripture; you will keep listeners' attention longer.
- Speak distinctly and don't rush through a sermon. It is better to leave listeners wanting than to talk fast and cover too many points. Younger people and older adults may have problems processing words spoken too quickly.

- End the sermon on time. Unless the Lord is moving in a mighty way, let his people go! Bodies that are hungry or thirsty have minds that don't listen. Bodies that are aching from sitting too long have minds that don't listen. Parents with tired and hungry children don't listen. All they are thinking about is the welfare of their children.

What Ministers Should Not Do

- Have fast-moving PowerPoints in which images and words flash, zoom, and whiz by.
- Have too many words on one slide.
- Have convoluted PowerPoints that jump all over the place.
- Have a disorganized message that jumps from one issue to another.
- Tell corny jokes—if you are not a funny person, don't try to come across as one.
- Share from your personal life when it doesn't apply to the message.
- Talk about what you've accomplished and what you are doing, and talk about it often. People don't care about you; they care about God working in your life.
- Play several videos during your message or videos that are too long. Short videos that serve a purpose are good, but if they go on too long, people wonder why they came to church, because they can watch a video at home. How long is too long? Five minutes.

Suggestions for Parents

Carolyn Brown is a Christian Education specialist and author who has written several books on the subject of having children in worship services. Here are some of her suggestions:

- Worship with rather than beside children.
- Stand children on the pew so that their ears, eyes, and mouths are near those of other worshipers as they sing, pray, and read together.
- Help young readers use hymnals and Bibles.
- Whisper instructions. "Now is the time we tell God about stuff we are sorry about." "Listen to this story. It is a good one."[2]

And a Little Child Led Them

In Oklahoma one Sunday, I was playing an arrangement of "Jesus Loves Me" for the offertory. This arrangement is based on "Clair de Lune," and it is contemplative and soothing. As the ushers finished passing the offering plates, I began to hear someone humming.

As I played softly I could hear this angelic voice as he began to sing the words. I looked down from the piano to see a little seven-year-old boy sitting all alone on the front row, drawing. Oblivious to the rest of the congregation, he began to sing softly from his heart. I extended the piece and kept playing. You could have heard a pin drop in that room as a hushed atmosphere took over. He would sing a few words and then hum a few bars. Tears began to flow down the faces of many adults in the congregation. It was indeed a spiritual moment as this little innocent child lifted our hearts toward the Savior.

Had this child been in a children's church, we would not have had the privilege of being blessed. That service belonged to our little friend, just like Matthew 11:25 says: "At that time Jesus said, 'I praise you, Father, Lord of heaven and earth, because you have hidden these things from the wise and learned, and revealed them to little children.'"

Ten Things Families Want in Family-Friendly Worship

1. Families with infants and toddlers want soft, friendly spaces.

2. Families with young children want their children to be acknowledged and engaged by church leadership.

3. Blended families want pews or rows large enough for all the children to sit together with the parents.

4. Single parents want a worship service where their children can be exposed to intergenerational help.

5. Single parents want a minister who upon preaching on marriage will give a disclaimer to the single parents to let them know the message also applies to them because they will need to teach their children about godly marriages.

6. Boomer families want music they can sing, so have the words available if they aren't familiar with the song.

7. Grandparents parenting again appreciate a children's church bulletin with activities such as fill-in-the-blanks so the grandchildren can participate in the service like the grandparent.

8. Boomerang families appreciate a mixture of contemporary praise music and hymns as they worship with the returning child and his or her parents.

9. Unchurched families want church terminologies and sacraments explained in words they can understand.

10. All families want to experience authentic worship led by leaders who are sincere, relational, relevant, and engaging.

Chapter 11

What to Do with Those Challenging Kids

I led them with cords of human kindness,
with ties of love;
To them I was like one who lifts
a little child to the cheek,
and I bent down to feed them.

—Hosea 11:4

More and more children with aggressive and challenging behaviors are showing up in churches. Church leaders and volunteers struggle to know how to work with these children. More than one leader has breathed a sigh of relief when a child with a challenging behavior or a "bad child" no longer shows up at their church.

Volunteers and leaders need to be trained in ministering and working with these children. These children with challenging behaviors include those with dysfunctional family situations and with special needs. These children can't just straighten up and act right.

Amy Fenton Lee, a leading expert in special needs ministry, says:

Bad behavior does not always reflect the state of a child's heart or even sin. In my interviews with education professional and intervention specialists, they repeatedly said that negative behavior is a means for communication rather than display of character deficiency. Prior to researching the topic of special needs inclusion, my natural inclination as a young parent and regular children's ministry volunteer was to quickly correct a disruptive child, to establish authority, and in some situations, allow the child to experience consequences for their poor choices.[1]

Unfortunately, many children's ministry volunteers still operate in the same mind-set as Amy describes. In her book Amy goes onto describe looking at these children through a different lens. I agree. We need to develop compassion and empathy for these children. We need to get training and learn about special needs children. Churches can open the door to the Kingdom for many children if only leaders, teachers, and volunteers learn how to accommodate these children.

When I train church ministry volunteers, I ask them what they would do if a child happened to show up with a broken arm in a cast. They usually say they would make accommodations for the child. When I ask them what they would do if a child in a wheelchair were in their children's group, they say, "We would accommodate the child." The same principal needs to apply to kids with challenging behaviors.

Several years ago when I was the DC4K (DivorceCare for Kids) consultant and trainer, a minister called me. His church was running the DC4K program. He was frustrated with a seven-year-old child's behavior and was going to ask him to leave, but the DC4K leaders had requested that he call me before he talked to the child's parent. He explained how out of control this child was. He said the child would run around the room yelling. He would climb on chairs and wouldn't join the rest of the group during circle time. He was obnoxious, and the other kids didn't like having him in the group. He said one time the child climbed on the table, raised his shirt, and said, "Look at my nipples," and then he started dancing on the table.

Our conversation went something like this:

Linda: Why are you going to kick a seven-year-old boy out of church?

Pastor: I'm not kicking him out of church. I'm asking him to leave the DC4K group.

Linda: Does the child attend any other program at your church? Because if he doesn't, then to the child you are kicking him out of church. Do you think this seven-year-old child will return to church when he is seventeen or twenty-seven or ever if he is kicked out at seven?

Pastor: You don't understand; he is out of control. What am I supposed to do?

Linda: Tell me,

- Who does the child live with?
- Who is the child's primary caregiver and does he go to day-care before and after school?
- How often does the child visit the other parent?
- What is the child's home life like?

Pastor: I don't know who he lives with or how often he visits the other parent. I have no idea who his primary caregiver is. I don't think he is in any other of our church classes, but I'm sure if he were, someone would have complained by now. I don't really know anything about this child except he is a wild child.

Linda: I can just about guarantee you this child doesn't feel safe. From what you have described, his behavior is crying out for some help. Some of his behavior might necessitate the calling of the authorities. First, I'd encourage you to find out the answers to the questions I've asked before you kick him out of church.

Pastor: I'm *not* kicking him out of church. I'll think about what you've said before doing anything.

When it comes to children, I'm not one to back off or let things slide, so in a few weeks I called this minister. Here is the gist of our conversation:

Linda: I've been praying for you and your seven-year-old friend. How is it going?

Pastor: You know, when I got off the phone with you last time I was really upset. I was determined no matter what you said I was going to ask the child to leave. But the Lord got a hold of me, and he wouldn't let me go. I started doing some digging, and here's what I found out.

- The child lives with his father, but his dad has to work long hours so he is rarely at home.
- The child stays with the grandmother before and after school and on many weekends.
- When he goes to visit his mom, I understand from the older sister that there are a lot of parties where there are drugs and alcohol. The little boy is made to dance on top of tables and everyone laughs at him.
- There doesn't appear to be much home life other than when he is at the grandmother's.

Here is what I did: I went to visit the grandmother, and she told me he gets into a lot of trouble at school and at home with his dad. But at her house he seems to feel safe. He obeys, is nurturing, and in general they have a good time together. So I asked the grandmother if she would consider coming to our DC4K and being one of our Safekeepers.[2] She now comes every week, and you know what? That child is in control, because I've learned he feels safe at DC4K. The teachers at school are reporting that his behavior at school is also coming into focus. We are making great strides with him, and all of our others kids now get to have a grandmother in our DC4K. It has turned out to be a win-win for all of us.

We like to think of childhood as a happy time for children. For millions of kids today that is not true. We used to think that if we just love them enough they will act like they are supposed to act.

In 2003 the Commission on Children at Risk did a research project to find out why so many children and youth were failing to flourish. This commission consisted of thirty-three leading children's doctors, research scientists, and youth service professionals. The report they issued is called "Hardwired to Connect."[3] The experts were also concerned with the large percentage of children and youth who were suffering from mental illness, emotional anguish, and overwhelming behavioral problems. This included but was not limited to depression and drug abuse, along with suicidal and violent tendencies. The majority of the people on the commission were children's doctors and those in the mental health profession. On page 8 the report says, "One of the main reasons we formed this commission is that our waiting lists are too long." The second reason members of the commission gave for developing this study is that society fails to understand the issues children face and professionals lack the ability to respond effectively to the decline of the well-being of America's children and youth.

The Hardwired to Connect study found the following to be of utmost concern for the well-being of the children in our communities:

- Our children are at risk and no one knows what to do or how to help them.
- Families are deteriorating while the churches are largely ignoring the problem.
- Communities have lost their ability to function as whole and viable places that protect their children and youth.

Basically what they discovered is that our children have a **poverty of connectedness**. The report shows two main outcomes:

1. Children are born with their brains hardwired for close connections to others. Children need to belong. Belonging is critical for their development.

2. Children are hardwired for spiritual meaning. This should be no surprise to those of us in the religious realm. We have known this for years but now it has been given credibility by scientists, doctors, and other professionals.

Is it any wonder that children in the following situations don't feel like they belong; don't have close connections; don't know if there is really a God?

- Divorce of parents
- Death of a parent
- Parents cohabitating (most of these situations are shaky at best, and the children usually end up seeing men and women parading through their lives)
- Living in a stepfamily that hasn't worked through the blending of two families
- Mental health issues in parents

What are church leaders and volunteers supposed to do when encountering children from these situations?

The Vacation Bible School Story

Right after I moved to Florida I had the opportunity to work in Vacation Bible School. The first day started out with the person in charge of our class saying,

"Okay, class, everyone sit over here against this wall. Josh, come over here with the rest of the group. Josh,[4] sit down. Josh, leave the paper on the wall alone. Josh! Stop that."

There is a heavy sigh after the teacher utters the last command.

It is my first day of VBS at my new church. I don't know the kids, the families, and I'm not real sure about the discipline policies. I am careful to observe other leaders' interactions. What I have learned so far is that some kids have been labeled as challenging. We've only been in VBS for a few minutes, and so far Josh has gotten all of the attention. Albeit negative attention; still it is attention. Not once has eye contact been made with Josh. Josh has succeeded in frustrating the teacher, alienating himself with the other kids, and has giggled throughout the entire process. Any part of this story sound familiar?[5]

Challenging Kids

I get that there are some children many of us don't want to deal with in our groups. Some of us might think if we didn't have Josh or Tia or Gavin or Lexi or whoever in our group everything would be fine. Things would run smoothly, and we could accomplish all of our goals. However, God created these children to be who they are, and it is our job to figure out how we can minister to each child God sends our way.

Even if a child has challenging behaviors, he or she still deserves for us as church leaders to give our best. To me, challenging is good. Challenging causes me to get creative. Challenging kids stretch me. Challenging forces me to rely on God's guidance. Challenging means praying without ceasing, something a lot of people working with challenging kids seem to forget.

Sometimes we forget to discipline so we punish instead. Discipline means to teach—to teach children how to act and let them know what we expect. Punishment means to enact a penalty or consequence for a wrong. Sometimes for adults who experience a "Josh," punishment can mean to exact revenge—maybe not consciously, but still we are all human and sometimes there are "those kids" who push our buttons.

If you ask questions about a particular child, you might hear:

- "I had him last year, and you have to let him know right away who is the boss."

- "He has a diagnosed behavior disorder."
- "He is on medication."
- "His parents let him get away with things."
- "You have to treat him with kid gloves or he throws a big fit and disrupts the entire group."
- "I had to call his mom one time. Big mistake!"

The list goes on and on. While it is important to understand specifics, what we don't need is adult judgments about something that has happened before. And I mean even the day before, let alone the year before. Each child deserves a fresh start every day.

Do We Set the Child Up to Fail?

When preparing for a new program, curriculum, or even a short-term project, it is important to think through the process of arrival beforehand:

- Is preregistration possible or does the child have to stand in a long line?
- Can a child go straight into a designated area or a room?
- Will the child need to mill around waiting for the adults to figure things out or fill out lengthy paperwork?

When we are not prepared in advance, many times we set a child up to fail. Insecurities and wondering what is going to happen can send some children into a tailspin.

Discipline is relationship specific. If you don't have a relationship with a child, and that includes knowing a child's last name, you can't expect to discipline him or her effectively. You can give directions or instructions, but it gets a little iffy when it comes to disciplining children. Many children who misbehave are actually seeking external regulation or management. In other words, they don't know how to internally regulate themselves so they seek outside regulation. Part of our job is providing that external regulation.

Children's behavior becomes their voice when they don't feel safe, don't feel loved, are confused, and don't know what is happening next. For many children, when they act out or misbehave, they are simply doing the best they can do to survive in that moment.

- Whirlwind behavior might be a cover-up for the intense pain the child feels. "If I keep busy, my heart won't hurt so much and I might forget my mom moved out."
- Disruptive actions might mean the child is operating from the lower levels of the brain—the fight, flight, or freeze part of the brain. When a child is in crisis, his or her brain can't think. This is the child who slides under the pew in the sanctuary or sits in the corner with his hoodie over his face.
- Aggressive children might be children who have lower levels of serotonin in the brain. Serotonin is a chemical in the brain that affects our emotional state. You might say it is the feel-good chemical. A crisis or trauma can impact the levels of serotonin being produced.
- For other children, acting out has become a habit. Or it has succeeded in getting them a lot of attention. In other words, it's been working for them. These are your class clowns. With these kids, go with the flow and use them to make your class enjoyable. Tuck them under your wing, so to speak, and let them burst forth when needed.

Simple Tips That Work for Most Children

- Preventative measures work best. Know in advance what you want the kids to do. Tell the children in as few words as possible. "We are going to play this next game outside. Then we will come back to our room for snack."

- Tell children what you want them to do. Refrain from telling them what you don't want them to do. Instead of, "No running in the hall," say, "Walk down the hall."
- Give children choices. Choices empower children who feel like they have no control over their lives.[6]
- Use the child's name as much as possible. Research tells us that hearing one's own name in everyday situations is an attention grabber. It causes a sudden rise in our own self-awareness. Using PET scans, researchers were able to see what happens in the brain when people hear their first name. There was an increase in blood flow to the part of the brain that plays a role in our processing of "self."[7]
- When requesting a child to do something, reframe how you make the request. Keep things simple by saying the child's name and the verb. "Ashley, sit down." "Alex, move over." "Cierra, quiet." "Roman, wait your turn."[8]
- Set boundaries. No matter what kids tell you, they like boundaries, structure, and predictability. Schedules are important and they lend to the feeling of safety, because schedules let a child know what is going to happen next. Post schedules.
- Apply the role of empathy in getting kids' attention. Patience, not punishment, turns angry students into happy kids. Kindness gets even angry teenagers' attention. Modeling kindness and empathy changes lives for the long term.[9]
- Use mirror neurons in the brain to change a child's mood. Mirror neurons allow what is happening in your brain to be projected onto other people. When you smile, it can activate the mirror neurons in another person's brain and they will mirror your expression. Just like a child catches a cold, kids can catch your mood.[10]
- Listen with your eyes. In other words, keep a watchful eye and notice what is going on at all times.

- Describe a child's action instead of praising a child. "Would you look at that! Samantha, you put the lids back on the markers." If a child has challenging behaviors, many times he or she can't handle praise. When praised she or he may set out to prove you wrong, so it is best to merely describe what the child did. If you feel you need to tag the action, say, "That was helpful." Please don't say, "Good job" or "Good boy." That is your judgment coming through.

- Children who have experienced a crisis or family trauma, such as divorce, are intuitive. They are people watchers. They have to be in order to survive in two separate households with different rules and expectations. These children will notice when you are judging them and they will shy away from any interactions with you.

- Does every infraction need to be addressed? Sometimes a look, nod of the head, or a hand signal will work effectively.[11]

In working with volunteers and leaders it is important to understand that changing the behavior of the children starts by changing the behavior of the adults. It may involve changing your mind-set, like Amy Fenton Lee; or trying to understand the child's living situation, like the minister who wanted to ask the seven-year-old to leave his church; or developing empathy; or using any one or all of the techniques listed above.

The Rest of the VBS Story

By the end of my first day of VBS, I had formed a relationship with Josh. I started by giving him choice after choice. "Josh, do you want to sit against that wall or over here with the group?" It really didn't make any difference to me if he sat alone.

I touched his shoulder gently when talking to him. I made eye contact. I smiled a lot. I prayed for him at every turn. I described his actions many times the first day. "Whoa, would you look at that. Josh was the first one to finish his project."

When we divided into small groups I made sure Josh was in my group. Then, I worked at building up his assets to the rest of the group. He really was a smart little kid, but because of his obnoxious behavior, the other kids shied away from him. By midweek the other boys were cheering him on during one of the races. Day by day you could see his self-worth escalating.

On Wednesday during music, he was tired and you could tell he was on the verge of an explosion. He didn't want to participate and refused to go on stage with the other kids. He was in the "challenge" mode. Not a problem for me because I love challenges.

I took a deep calming breath, put on my calmest stance, slowly walked toward him with a smile on my face and said, "Josh, you don't have to go on the stage. However, I can't allow you to be a distraction to the other kids. You can stand by the piano or you can sit on one of these pews. What's your choice?" He said, "I don't want to be here. I want to go home" to which I replied in a soft, firm but nurturing voice, "Bummer! Going home is not a choice. Now, do you want to stand by the piano or choose a pew to sit in?" Josh, "Oh, okay. I'll stand by the piano."[12]

When we finished the weeklong session all was good. Josh felt better about himself. The other kids had accepted him, and Mom wasn't called all week to intervene.

Chapter 12

More Help Attracting Families to Your Church

From him the whole body, joined and held together by every
supporting ligament, grows and builds itself up in love,
as each part does its work.

—Ephesians 4:16

There are many ways to reach out and attract families to your church. Perhaps God has already impressed upon your heart the type of families he wants you to bring into your church. Maybe while reading through this book you've thought of people in your church family who are waiting to be asked to serve alongside you.

We know most people in our world today don't have extra time or energy to devote to one more cause. So don't make serving the church a cause:

- Make it easy.
- Keep it simple.
- Make it natural.
- Keep it focused.
- Make it family.

Church leadership might decide the first step is gathering the church family together and finding out what their stories are. This is not a gathering for everyone to list his or her complaints, but one of testifying, rejoicing, praying, and assessing what God is doing in the lives of families in your own church. Listen to those stories. In those stories you will find passion, sincerity, and a natural call to serve.

Churches wanting to attract new people and families to their church could take a page out of the secular world. Think about what happened after the Oklahoma City bombing; after 9/11; after Hurricane Katrina; and after the worst tornado in history, an F5, hit Moore, Oklahoma, in the spring of 2013:

- Neighbors reached out to one another out of concern.
- Strangers jumped in immediately to help the trapped and injured.
- Hurting people looked for other hurting people who were feeling the same kind of pain they were experiencing.
- Encouraging words were spoken.
- Hope was given.
- Prayers were prayed.
- Money was donated to help those in need.
- Community was formed among strangers.

In Moore, Oklahoma, when the tornado hit the Plaza Towers Elementary School, people came running down the street to help the children. Until the first responders could get there, strangers pulled injured children and teachers out of that school. Why did they do this? They did it because they were concerned for the welfare of the children. Many, without thinking about it, ran and started digging and pulling out the children. They didn't stop to think about the danger to themselves; they only thought about the children buried under the heavy rubble. The panic and the urgency of the situation prompted strangers, first responders, friends, and family to act. Lives were saved. The injured were taken to hospitals where their wounds were treated.

Let me ask you:

- Shouldn't those of us in the church do and feel the same way about lost souls?
- Why aren't we digging out the children buried under the rubble of the world? The world weighs heavy upon their souls.
- Where are the first responders in the church?
- The disciples and those serving in the New Testament church must have felt the urgency to serve the risen Savior. They went from place to place preaching the gospel. They created and encouraged a community of believers.

Care and Support Ministries: A Bridge to Your Church

By listening to the stories of people in your church, you will find people who are willing to comfort someone with the comfort they themselves received. You will find servants who will be willing to serve in ministries that will be a bridge to your church. I know for myself in my younger years, I never thought about serving in a divorce recovery ministry. Actually, I was indignant about divorce. I thought couples that divorced hadn't tried hard enough. I was offended that Christian couples would even think about divorce. My attitude was divorce is wrong—that is, until my husband walked out on me. I didn't want a divorce. I prayed, begged, pleaded, went to counseling, and refused to get my own lawyer, but no matter what I thought or did, the divorce went through.

I now have a passion to help struggling marriages. I don't want anyone to experience a divorce. For those who do experience a divorce, I want to help and encourage them because God is not through with them and there is life after divorce. They can discover new talents and gifts that can be used in service to God. I want them to know God still loves them. I'm not a minister or a trained counselor.

I am an individual who wants to serve God, and there are many just like me sitting in the pews of your church.

Bridge ministries are just that, a means of allowing people in your community an avenue to get to your church. They can take on many forms. These ministries can include but are not limited to the following:

- Ministries to those with addictive behaviors
- Life crisis ministries, such as for divorce or the death of a loved one
- Ministries to keep fathers involved. This could be a men's ministry or some other creative ministry, such as a men's moving ministry or a fix-it ministry where men repair homes.
- Parenting alone classes to help men and women parent their children as single parents
- Military ministries to support the deployed, their return, and reuniting with family
- Special needs ministries to children with special needs
- Foster care ministries where families in your church are encouraged to be full-time foster parents or emergency foster care parents
- Marriage ministries to save marriages on the brink of divorce

The ministry for some of your congregants might be sharing the difficulties and successes of blending a second marriage. Another person might excel in working with the older populations in your neighborhood. Foster families can mentor others to become foster parents.

The possibilities are limited only by the human mind.

As our world continue to spin faster and faster, I believe God has ministries in mind that our limited human brains can't even begin to comprehend at this time. As we pray and search, God will reveal to each church what its role should be in its community, just as he says he will in Ephesians: "Now to him who is able to do immeasurably more than all we ask or imagine, according to his power that is at work within us, to him be glory in the church and Christ Jesus throughout all generations, for ever and ever! Amen"(Ephesians 3:20-21).

Notes

1. The Church That Might Have Been

1. David T. Olson, *The American Church in Crisis* (Grand Rapids: Zondervan, 2008), 181.

2. Ibid., 25.

3. Thom Shultz, "5 Ways the Church Will Change," *Holy Soup* (blog), November 14, 2012, http://holysoup.com/2012/11/14/5-ways-the-church -will-change/.

4. John Burke, "Growth in the Gutter," *Christianity Today*, Spring 2009, http://www.christianitytoday.com/le/2009/spring/growinginthegutter .html.

5. Ed Stetzer and Thom S. Rainer, *Transformational Church: Creating a New Scorecard for Congregations* (Nashville: B & H, 2010), 34.

6. Patrick F. Fagan and Robert Rector, "The Effects of Divorce on America," The Heritage Foundation, last modified June 5, 2000, accessed November 22, 2013, http://www.heritage.org/research/reports/2000/06 /the-effects-of-divorce-on-america.

7. Schultz, "5 Ways the Church Will Change."

8. Olson, *The American Church in Crisis*, 135.

2. What Parents Want

1. Greg Baird, "What Families Want from Church," *KidMin360* (blog), http://kidmin360.com/what-families-want-from-church/.

2. An excellent and complete safety checklist can be found and down-loaded free from Jill B. Carter, *Protecting Our Church and Children: What Church Leaders Must Know*, http://www.ncbaptist.org/fileadmin/ministries /children/resources/2013/pdfs/files/protecting-church-children-new.pdf.

3. See KidCheck, a web-based children's check-in solution for churches: www.kidcheck.com.

4. "Reducing the Risk," *Christianity Today*, accessed November 21, 2013, http://www.reducingtherisk.com/?utm_source=childrensministry-html& utm_medium=Newsletter&utm_term=5535554&utm_content= 145396397&utm_campaign=2012.

5. Matt McKee, "Family Church Collaborate," in *Collaborate: Family + Church*, ed. Ross Brodfuehrer et al. (Louisville: Ministers Label, 2010), ch. 22.

6. Mark Steiner, "Choosing a Children's Curriculum," *DiscipleBlog .com* (blog), December 20, 2012, http://www.discipleblog.com/2012/12 /childrens-curriculum//.

7. Elizabeth Marquardt et al., "The President's Marriage Agenda for the Forgotten Sixty Percent," *The State of Our Unions* (Charlottesville, VA: National Marriage Project and Institute for American Values, 2012), xii, http://stateofourunions.org/2012/SOOU2012.pdf.

8. Katelyn Beaty, "Why Middle-Class Marriages Need the Church," *FamilyScholars.org* (blog), December 20, 2012, http://familyscholars.org /2012/12/20/why-middle-class-marriages-need-the-church/.

9. Marquardt et al., "The President's Marriage Agenda," xi.

10. See Choosing Wisely Before You Divorce, http://www.beforeyou divorce.org/.

11. Baird, "What Families Want from Church."

3. Taking a Page out of the Book of Nehemiah

1. See Church Census, http://www.baylor.edu/social_work/cfcm/index .php?id=66788.

2. Franci Rogers, "What Church Families Want," *Family and Community Ministries*, http://www.baylor.edu/content/services/document.php /145215.pdf.

3. Carmella is not her real name.

4. Church Census.

5. Mike MacManus, "How to Restore Marriage in N.C.: How to Rebuild the Marriage Culture," *Family North Carolina*, 3, http://ncfamily.org /FNC/1302-FNC-Restoring%20Marriage.pdf.

6. Andy Patterson, October 23, 2012 (3:12 p.m.), comment on post by Linda Ranson Jacobs (October 23, 2012, 3:02 p.m.) on Family Ministry Church Leader's Facebook page.

7. See "What Is Operation Inasmuch?," Operation Inasmuch, accessed October 18, 2013, http://operationinasmuch.org/about/.

4. Creating a Family-Friendly Church for Single-Parent Families

1. Jena is not her real name.

2. Rosa is not her real name.

3. Chuck is not his real name.

4. "Children in Single-Parent Families," Kids Count Data Center, accessed October 18, 2013, http://datacenter.kidscount.org/data/acrossstates /Rankings.aspx?ind=106.

5. Jennifer Wolf, "Single Parent Statistics," *About.com*, accessed October 18, 2013, http://singleparents.about.com/od/support/p/single_parent _statistics_us.htm.

6. "Data by Location," Kids Count Data Center, accessed October 18, 2013, http://datacenter.kidscount.org/locations.

7. Jennifer Barnes Maggio, *The Church and the Single Mom* (Stone Mountain, GA: CarePoint Ministry, 2011), 42.

8. Theresa McKenna, *The Hidden Mission Field: Caring for Single Parent Families in the 21st Century* (Mukilteo, WA: WinePress Publishing, 1999).

9. Patrick F. Fagan, "The Impact of Marriage and Divorce on Children," The Heritage Foundation, last modified May 13, 2004, http://www.heritage .org/research/testimony/the-impact-of-marriage-and-divorce-on-children.

10. Michael Price, "Suicide Among Pre-adolescents," *Monitor on Psychology* 49, no. 9 (October 2010): 52, https://www.apa.org/monitor /2010/10/suicide.aspx.

11. Claudia Jewett Jarratt, *Helping Children Cope with Separation and Loss* (Boston: Harvard Common Press, 1994).

12. Patrick F. Fagan and Robert Rector, "The Effects of Divorce on America," The Heritage Foundation, last modified June 5, 2000, accessed November 22, 2013, http://www.heritage.org/research/reports/2000/06 /the-effects-of-divorce-on-america.

13. Elizabeth Marquardt, *Between Two Worlds: The Inner Lives of Children of Divorce* (New York: Crown, 2005), 10.

14. Read more about the three stages of single parenting at Healthy Loving Partnerships for Our Kids, "Articles," http://www.hlp4.com/articles .html.

15. See DivorceCare, www.divorcecare.org.

16. See GriefShare, www.griefshare.org.

17. See DivorceCare for Kids, www.dc4k.org.

18. Trisha McCary Rhoades, *The Soul at Rest* (Minneapolis: Bethany House Publishers, 1996).

19. Doug Dees, "Partnering Parents," in *Baker Handbook of Single Parent Ministry*, ed. Bobbie Reed (Grand Rapids: Baker Books, 1998), 244.

20. Rob Reinow, "Bible Driven Ministry to Single Parents" (2012), http://visionaryfam.com/wp-content/uploads/2012/09/Bible-Driven-Ministry-to-Single-Parents.pdf.

21. Linda Ranson Jacobs, "Ten Things You Need to Know to Minister to Children of Divorce," *DivorceMinistry4Kids.com* (blog), January 12, 2013, http://DivorceMinistry4Kids.com/2013/10-things-you-need-to-know-to-minister-to-children-of-divorce/.

22. Linda Ranson Jacobs, "10 Ways to Pray for Children of Divorce and Their Families," *DivorceMinistry4Kids.com* (blog), January 18, 2013, http://DivorceMinistry4Kids.com/2013/10-ways-to-pray-for-children-of-divorce-and-their-families/.

5. Nontraditional Families Are the New Normal

1. Ron L. Deal, "Marriage, Family, and Stepfamily Statistics," Smart-Stepfamilies, last modified March 2013, http://www.smartstepfamilies.com/view/statistics.

2. Ibid.

3. Moe and Paige Becnel, in e-mail interview by author, March 21, 2013. See www.blendingafamily.com.

4. Ron L. Deal is Director of Blended Family Ministries at FamilyLife, http://www.SmartStepfamilies.com.

5. From the description for *Ministering to Stepfamilies* (DVD) by Ron Deal, http://shop.familylife.com/p-1818-ministering-to-stepfamilies-dvd.aspx.

6. Moe and Paige Becnel (interview). See Moe and Paige Becnel, *God Breathes on Blended Families* (Castle Rock, CO: Blending a Family Ministry, 2009).

7. Jeff Parziale, Home Page, In Step Ministries, accessed January 2013, http://www.instepministries.com. This quotation has since been removed from the website.

8. Linda Ranson Jacobs, "One Child, Two Homes," *Thriving Family*, September/October 2010, http://www.thrivingfamily.com/Family/Life/Blended%20Family/2010/sep/one-child-two-homes.aspx.

9. United States Census Bureau, "Facts for Features," last modified July 31, 2012, http://www.census.gov/newsroom/releases/archives/facts_for_features_special_editions/cb12-ff17.html.

10. To find such a group in your area, see DivorceCare for Kids, http://www.dc4k.org/findagroup.

11. Emanuella Grinberg, "College Grads and Their Families Learn to Live Together," CNN.com, last modified June 27, 2012, http://www.cnn.com/2012/06/26/living/college-grads-moving-home/index.html.

12. Steve Johnson, "Singles (Even without Kids) Are Part of the Family Ministry," *Etchea Coaching* (blog), March 12, 2013, http://etchea.com/singles-even-without-kids-are-part-of-family-ministry/.

13. Kris Swiatocho, "Why My Church Doesn't Have a Singles Ministry," *Pastors.com* (blog), July 31, 2012, http://pastors.com/why-my-church-doesnt-have-a-singles-ministry/.

14. Johnson, "Singles."

6. Other Common Family Structures

1. Judith Wallerstein, Julia M. Lewis, and Sandra Blakeslee, *The Unexpected Legacy of Divorce: A 25 Year Landmark Study* (New York: Hyperion, 2000).

2. Elizabeth Marquardt, *Between Two Worlds: The Inner Lives of Children of Divorce* (New York: Crown, 2005), 135.

3. Linda Jacobs, "What Adult Children of Divorce Want Church Leaders to Know," *DivorceCare for Kids Blog* (blog), June 6, 2013, http://blog.dc4k.org/?p=622.

4. For this quotation and the next three, see ibid.

5. Jen Abbas, *Generation Ex: Adult Children of Divorce and the Healing of Our Pain* (Little Rock: FamliyLife, 2006), 49.

6. The majority of this section was from personal interviews with adult children of divorce.

7. DivorceCare for Kids, http://www.dc4k.org, is a support ministry for children of divorce.

8. Robyn Besemann, *Chained No More Leader Guide* (Bloomington, IN: WestBow Press, 2012), iii. See http://robynbministries.com/chainednomore.

9. Jim Toedtman, "The Magic of the Fountain of Youth," *AARPBulletin* (January/February 2013), 3.

10. Thom S. Rainer, "Last Chances for Churches to Reach 50 Million Americans," *ThomRainer.com* (blog), January 28, 2013, http://thomrainer.com/2013/01/28/last-chances-for-churches-to-reach-50-million-americans/#.UVuWgELi6JU.

11. Eric Nagourney, "Why Am I Back in Church?," NTTimes.com, last modified October 3, 2012, http://www.nytimes.com/2012/10/04/booming/04question-booming.html.

12. Ibid.

13. Ibid.

14. James Craver, First Baptist Church Allen, Associate Pastor, 201 E. McDermott, Allen, Texas 75002, 972-727-8241, james.craver@fbcallen .org. See www.fbcallen.org.

15. James Craver, phone call to author, April 2, 2013.

16. Robert Hughes Jr., "Are Boomers Still Pushing Up the Divorce Rate?," *HuffPost* (blog), November 2, 2012, http://www.huffingtonpost .com/robert-hughes/are-baby-boomers-still-pu_b_2012199.html.

17. Carrie Gann, "Sex Life of Older Adults and Rising STDs," *ABC News Health* (blog), February 3, 2012, http://abcnews.go.com/blogs /health/2012/02/03/older-people-getting-busy-and-getting-stds/.

18. Matthew Brown, "Religion May Play More Prominent Role in America as Baby Boomers Age," *Deseret News* Online, last modified December 29, 2012, www.deseretnews.com/article/865569639/Religion-may-play -more-prominent-role-in-America-as-baby-boomers-age.html?pg=all.

7. Looks Count and So Do Church Attitudes

1. For information about Will Mancini's consultant work, which includes mystery worshiper possibilities, see "Why Auxano?," last modified 2012, http://www.willmancini.com/wp-content/uploads/2010/05/why-use -auxano-church-consulting.pdf.

2. Geoff Surratt, "5 Simple Ways to Make Your Church Stickier," *ChurchLeaders.com* (blog), http://www.churchleaders.com/outreach-mis sions/outreach-missions-blogs/158310-geoff_surratt_five_simple_ways _to_make_your_church_stickier_part_1.html.

8. Keeping the Family in Family Ministry

1. Rob Rienow, *Limited Church: Unlimited Kingdom* (Nashville: Randall House, 2013), 259–64.

2. Kenneth Conley, "Faith Is Supposed to Be Messy," *ChildrensMinistryOnline.com* (blog), January 21, 2013, http://childrensministryonline .com/family/faith-is-supposed-to-be-messy/.

3. Christine Yount Jones, "Trend Quakes," ChildrensMinistry.com, accessed October 18, 2013, http://childrensministry.com/articles/trend -quakes.

4. David T. Olson, *The American Church in Crisis* (Grand Rapids: Zondervan, 2008), 161.

5. Wayne Stocks, "Does the Shape of Families Shape Faith?" *Divorce-Ministry4Kids.com* (blog), January 10, 2013, http://DivorceMinistry4Kids .com/2013/does-the-shape-of-families-shape-faith/.

6. Linda Ranson Jacobs, "Children of Divorce Deserve Better Treatment in Our Churches," FamilyScholars.org, last modified January 17, 2013, http://familyscholars.org/2013/01/17/children-of-divorce-deserve -better-treatment-in-our-churches/.

7. Dick Gruber, "Families Serving Together," in *Collaborate Family + Church*, ed. Ross Brodfuehrer et al. (Louisville: Ministers Label, 2010), 48. This is a book of collaborative effort with thirty-five contributing authors.

8. See Orange, http://www.whatisorange.org/.

9. Reggie Joiner, *Think Orange: Imagine the Impact When Church and Family Collide* (Colorado Springs, CO: David C. Cook, 2009).

10. Andy Stanley, foreword to ibid.

11. See "Family Ministry Blog Tour Posts," http://itspastormatt .com/?page_id=349.

12. Eric Wallace, *Uniting Church and Home: A Blueprint for Rebuilding Church Community* (Lorton, VA: Solutions for Integrating Church and Home, 1999), 75.

9. Electronic Steeples

1. Albert Mohler, *The Conviction to Lead: 25 Principles for Leadership That Matters* (Minneapolis: Bethany House Publishers, 2012), 177.

2. See Church Initiative, http://www.churchinitiative.org/. Church Initiative is the developer of DivorceCare, DC4K, GriefShare, Single and Parenting, and other outreach ministries for churches.

3. Information comes from a business seminar hosted by the *Pensacola News Journal* for local businesses and evaluations of business websites.

4. BusinessNewsDailyStaff, "The Seven Most Important Things on Your Website," *Business News Daily* Online, February 16, 2012, http://www.businessnewsdaily.com/2046-web-design-data.html.

5. Charles Stone, "Maximizing Ministry with Your iPad: Learn How to Enhance Your Ministry with Your iPad," Stonewell Ministries, accessed October 18, 2013, http://charlesstone.com/wp-content/uploads/2013/08/MaximizingMinistryWithYouriPad.pdf.

6. See Leadercast, http://www.chick-fil-aleadercast.com.

7. Todd McKeever, "Using Skype and Live Minutes in Children's Ministry," *iTodd* (blog), January 23, 2013, http://www.toddmckeever.com/2013/01/using-skype-and-live-minutes-in-childrens-ministry/.

8. "Learn about Skype," Skype, http://beta.skype.com/en/what-is-skype/.

9. Live Minutes, http://liveminutes.com.

10. See Roar, http://roar.pro/#. Roar is a social media consulting group. Their concentration is on helping churches. They can develop a church app, set up your website, and provide an array of other services geared toward helping your church go digital.

11. Summer Pridemore, "Social Media in Church Survey Results [Infographic]," *Roar Blog* (blog), January 29, 2013, http://roar.pro/social-media-in-church-survey-results-infographic/.

12. Matt McKee with Joni Tapp, *Be Social: The Social Media Handbook for Churches* (2011).

13. Todd McKeever, "Facebook and Twitter in Children's Ministry," *CMConnect.org* (blog), January 22, 2013, http://my.cmconnect.org/profiles/blogs/facebook-and-twitter-in-children-8217-s-ministry. You can find more from Todd at iTodd, http://www.toddmckeever.com/.

10. Making Worship Family Friendly

1. Melanie Gordon, "A Family-Friendly Church—Issue #143," GBOD.org, last modified 2012, http://www.gbod.org/lead-your-church/best-practices-romans-12/resource/a-family-friendly-church-a-issue-143.

2. Carolyn C. Brown, *You Can Preach to the Kids, Too!: Designing Sermons for Adults and Children* (Nashville: Abingdon Press, 1997), 109.

11. What to Do with Those Challenging Kids

1. Amy Lee Fenton, *Leading Special Needs Ministry: A Practical Guide to Including Children and Loving Families* (n.p.: Orange, 2013).

2. DC4K leaders are called Safekeepers. It is a term that conveys that children are safe at DC4K. Dr. Becky Bailey coined the phrase in the Conscious Discipline book and program. See Conscious Discipline, http://con sciousdiscipline.com.

3. See a summary of *Hardwired to Connect: The Scientific Case for Authoritative Communities* at "Reports," Institute for American Values, http:// www.americanvalues.org/html/hardwired_-_ex_summary.html.

4. Josh is not his real name.

5. Linda Ranson Jacobs, "Hey! Stop That! Discipline Techniques That Work," KidzMatter.com January/February 2013, http://awana.org/on/de mandware.store/Sites-kidzmatter-Site/default/Page-Show?cid=kmag-jf13 -discipline.

6. For more on this subject, see Linda Ranson Jacobs, "Empowering Children through Choices," Church Initiative, June 24, 2013, http://www .scribd.com/doc/149733645/Empowering-Children-Through-Choices.

7. F. Perrin et al., "Neural Mechanisms Involved in the Detection of Our First Name: A Combined ERPs and PET Study," *Neuropsychologia* 43, no. 1 (2005): 12–19.

8. For more on reframing what we say to children, see Linda Ranson Jacobs, "Oh Those Challenging Kids—What to Say, Not to Say, and How to Say It," *DivorceMinistry4Kids.com* (blog), April 20, 2012, http://divorce ministry4kids.com/2012/oh-those-challenging-kids-what-to-say-not-to -say-and-how-to-say-it/.

9. A great example of this principle can be found in Jane Ellen Stevens, "Lincoln High School in Walla Walla, WA, Tries New Approach to School Discipline—Suspensions Drop 85%," *ACES Too High News*, April 23, 2012, http://acestoohigh.com/2012/04/23/lincoln-high-school-in-walla -walla-wa-tries-new-approach-to-school-discipline-expulsions-drop-85/.

10. For more on this subject, see Linda Ranson Jacobs, "The Incredible Amazing Brain in Children of Divorce," *DivorceMinistry4Kids.com* (blog), January 20, 2012, http://divorceministry4kids.com/2012/the-incredible -amazing-brain-in-children-of-divorce/.

11. Jacobs, "Hey! Stop That!"

12. Ibid.

Made in the USA
Lexington, KY
18 December 2014